Rainy Day Press

TRACKING DOWN COYOTE

Mike Helm grew up in Pendleton, Oregon, where he learned to ride horses and harvest peas and wheat. During the Vietnam War he served in the Marine Corps in California and the Peace Corps in Uganda and Kenya. He holds degrees from Oregon State University and the University of Oregon and currently lives with his family in Eugene, Oregon, where he teaches writing and literature in the International High School. His first book was a guidebook for Eugene. He compiled and edited *Conversations with Pioneer Women, Conversations with Bullwhackers, Muleskinners, Etc., A Bit of Verse,* and *Visionaries , Mountain Men & Empire Builders.* His most recent book is *Oregon's Ghosts and Monsters.* (Rainy Day Press, 1985)

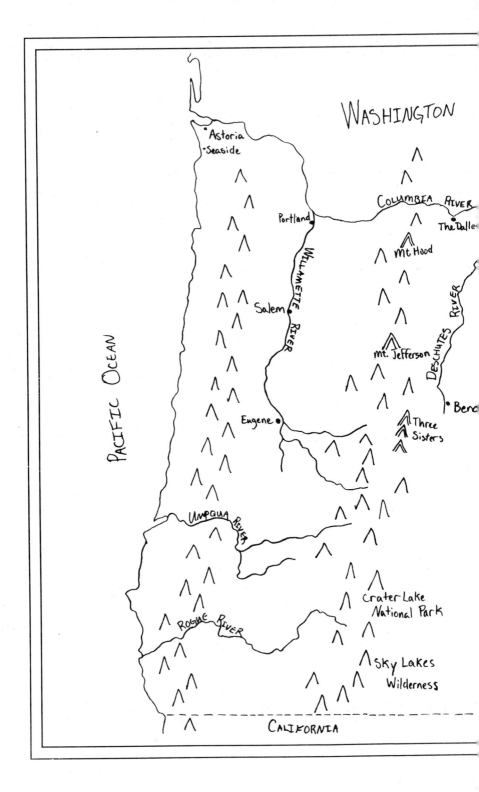

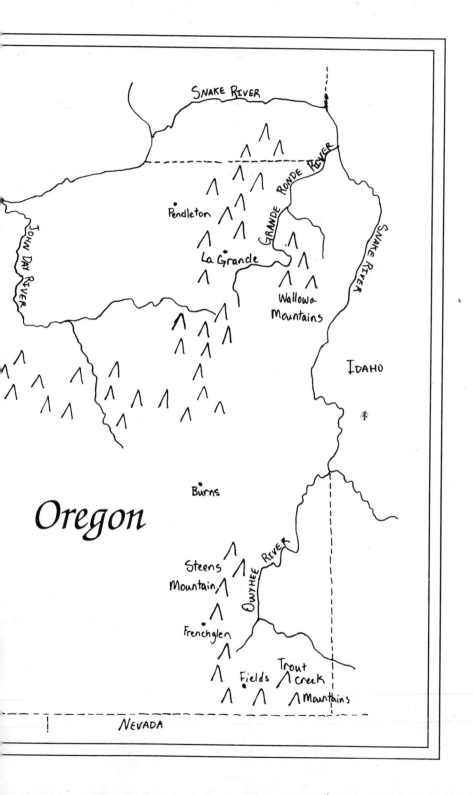

For
Chris, Ben, Malindi,
Polly and Luke

Tracking Down Coyote

Mike Helm

First Edition
Published in October, 1990

Copyright © by Rainy Day Press, 1990
Illustrations copyright © by Polly Helm, 1990

Library of Congress Catalog Card Number
85-071554

International Standard Book Number
0-931742-16-1

Published by Rainy Day Press
PO Box 3035
Eugene, Oregon 97403

Printed in the United States of America
Lino-cut illustrations by Polly Helm
Maps by Chris Helm and Polly Helm
Book design by Mike Helm
The type is Palatino.

Table of Contents

Who is to say what wonder we will discover when we become aware of what lies invisible about us. Perhaps the air is full of shades. Perhaps there are layers and layers of history living right here, dimension piled upon dimension—the past like curtains hung in rows—like the gauzy greenness of the northern lights. What do you think of that?

W. P. Kinsella
"Frank Pierce, Iowa"

In the Beginning...

I had this fantasy of spending ten days or so with no roof over my head, so, a week or so before I left I took the top off the Jeep and stashed it in the shop.

"Aren't you even taking a tent?" Chris asked, shaking her head. Nope. I was going to the desert. In the summer.

"What about the top for the Jeep?" Polly said. Nope. But I changed my mind on that. After all, the sun might get a little too hot. The night before I left I folded the top tight and stuffed it into the Jeep behind the box I'd built to hold my camping gear. Thursday morning came warm and sunny. I kissed the kids and Chris goodbye and headed off across the Cascades in my topless Jeep.

At the far end of Springfield I stopped and bought my usual camping supplies—a few cans of chili and a couple of cans of spaghetti and some chips and fruit—and a couple of last-minute items at BiMart and Safeway and then I was off, up and over the Cascades and onto the desert. Not a cloud in the sky and, certainly no clouds in my sky because I'd just signed the papers on a house refinance that I'd worked for more than two years to accomplish. This was a celebration trip, a trip I'd been dreaming about since March when we were all here for spring vacation.

I gassed up in Bend and then headed for Burns. The wind and the sun were my companions in my topless Jeep and I felt wild and free, absolutely exhilarated as we hummed across the desert. About the time I passed Millican, though, I could feel the sun burning through my thinning hair and when I looked at myself in the rear view mirror a red-faced person looked back. For protection, I dug out my old floppy green hat, which was promptly blown off by the blast from a passing truck. I retrieved it and held it on with my hand from then on.

Seven or eight miles east of Hampton a road heads off south through the desert. This is the same road we used in the Blue Goose when we came through in March. We followed it for a few miles, till we were just south of Glass Butte and camped for the night. It was mid-afternoon when I arrived at the turn-off and I remembered a couple of old cabins that I wanted to photograph, so I retraced our spring break route, towing a huge plume of white dust behind me. I knew, too, that the route of the Meek Wagon Train of 1845, which I intended to research during this trip, passed just east of Glass Butte, running north from Lost Hollow on the north end of Wagontire Mountain and I thought I would try to retrace that part of the route, driving on Jeep roads southeast across the desert to Wagontire Mountain.

I found and photographed the two homesteads we saw during spring break, then continued down the same road past our previous campsite. Four or five miles out in the sagebrush, I came to a crossroad and what must have been a fairly extensive ranch. Part of what I judged to be the original cabin was made of juniper logs, with one low window. From there it was easy to trace the development of the place, as the extension of the juniper cabin was made with boards. Later, the cabin was used as a barn and another house was built, this one of lumber and shingles and an August, 1935 *San Francisco Examiner* for wallpaper. "Amateur Golf Tourney Lures Babe Ruth," and "An End to Romance the Nazis Disapproved," the walls said. Screens covered the windows in the good old days, but they were torn, the windows shot out or broken with rocks. Every board was gray and weathered, desert driftwood. Corrals, some made of juniper logs, some of boards, and some of lodgepole pine and barbed wire, sprawled north and east from the little collection of buildings and led, through a maze of gates, to a sturdy juniper-log loading ramp near the road.

There is so much evidence of human activity in such a place that I expect to hear voices, doors slamming, engines starting. I am an intruder, a burglar, prying into private places as I walk through the house, and, though I know I'm alone, there's a part of me that's apprehensive, feels like I might stumble into the bedroom and find someone still there, sleeping, shocked at my intrusion. Jackrabbits and mice scurry away at the sound of my footsteps.

Outside, there are no cows, no trucks, no cowboys. My Jeep sits in the middle of the road and blocks no traffic. A mile or so down the road a plume of dust slides noiselessly toward the old house. For a minute it is a rancher, curious about my intrusion, but it swirls off the road, dances through the sagebrush, thins and disappears.

But such places, wild places, (though they might once have been tame) are alive with all that has happened in them. I imagine children running and tussling just outside the house, their mother tidying inside, reading the walls,—"Amateur Golf Tourney Lures Babe Ruth"—watching over them through the windows. Tumbleweeds and dust devils and rabbits play there now. Birds and wind are the only sound. In such places, spirits abound.

You see, in the beginning...

The world was made by Old Man Above, who sat on a stool while engaged in his work of creation. When he finished he made the fish and the animals and then man. It was man's job to determine the rank and duties of all the animals. He decided to give each of the animals a bow and some arrows. To the more important animals he would give the longer bows.

Coyote, of course, thought he deserved the longest bow, and he decided to stay awake all night so he could be first at the distribution, which was to occur the following morning. Toward midnight, when his eyelids were heavy with sleep, he put twigs in his eyes to prop them open. Later, so he would be fresh and alert when he appeared before man in the morning, Coyote decided to sleep for just a short while. He pulled the twigs out of his eyes and fell sound asleep. When he awoke, the sun was high in the sky and, instead of being first at the distribution, he was last. By the time he arrived there was only one bow left, the shortest and poorest of them all.

Man felt sorry for Coyote and asked Old Man Above for advice. Because he, too, sympathized with Coyote, Old Man Above decreed that Coyote should be the most cunning of all the animals, and that is the way it has been ever since.[1]

Coyote is Oregon's mightiest spirit. He dug the Columbia Gorge, created Clatsop Spit, placed the mountains and coastal rocks, and built the waterfalls. He created the tribes, taught the people to make babies, vanquished monsters that preyed on them, and gave them the salmon. But much has happened since Coyote built and peopled Oregon and now other spirits, too, share our wild places.

In the Wallowa Mountains you might camp, as we did, beneath a pine tree near the Minam River. The tree has sheltered many campers in its 250 years, and once, not so many years ago as trees reckon time, Old Chief Joseph passed this spot, rested for a night, leaned against that very tree as you do now. Later, snug in your sleeping bag, look for a moment into the smoke of your campfire. Listen carefully to the night sounds. Look and listen with your heart and you will see and hear the Indians who called these mountains home a thousand years before the white men drove them away. They are here, as surely as you are.

In 1845 Stephen Meek led 200 wagons, 1000 people, with their cattle, goats, and dogs out across the Oregon desert. A shortcut, he told them, to the Willamette Valley. Can't you see them through the heat waves stolidly moving west? Listen. On the wind you will hear the creak of harness leather, the muffled curses of the bullwhackers, even old Sam Parker as he leaves the hot springs at Vale that August day: *"tuck what is caled the meeks Cut of misses Butts tuck Sick this day"* Later, he added: *"A Bad Cut of fore all that tuck it"*

Wild places resonate with spirits. You can hear them in the wind and see them in the sky. You will recognize them in the cry of a goose on a clear fall morning, the wail of a coyote at sunset. Listen. You can hear the voice of the trapper and the Indian and the pioneer and the sound of the plow turning over the bunchgrass and starting a farm in Oregon. If you look ever so carefully, you will see three-toed horses and woolly mammoths grazing in the Oregon Desert and stone-age hunters, sandal-makers, huddled in caves where coyotes now raise their pups.

That's what this book is about—tracking down Coyote, the spirit of Oregon's wild places.

I should confess that there has been for me only one life-long love affair, and that has been with Oregon. It began as soon as I was old enough to take note of my surroundings and I don't suppose it will ever die.

Long ago, my father taught me to bait a hook, to shoot straight, and where all the backroads led. The Blue Mountains and their vast, rolling foothills were our playground. We had a big canvas tent and a 1947 Buick. Weekends found us beside one stream or another, where the fish, at least for my father, were always biting.

Old photographs show us posed on the front lawn with the bounty of our hunting and fishing trips. We ate what was in season: trout nearly year-round, steelhead in the spring, salmon in the summer, pheasant and venison in the fall, duck and goose in the winter. Once, when he had been hunting without me, my father came home with a load of geese, one in

5

a gunny sack. A swan, he explained nervously. That night, on the table, it looked like a big goose.

Because my mother's family spent part of each summer at the beach, we did too. When I was very young we went to Seaside—where, years later, she died—and then to Tolovana Park, just south of Cannon Beach. With her I first smelled the ocean and heard the surf. We walked the beaches and built sand castles for the tide to wash away. She taught me about hermit crabs and sea anemones and the myriad creatures the tide leaves behind. My father, always the predator, taught me to pry mussels from the rocks, dig razor clams from the beach, and fish in the surf.

These two ends of the state—rolling foothills and mountains in the east, rocky headlands, beaches and ocean in the west—were the boundaries of my childhood. They stood like bookends on a shelf, and between them we fished, hunted, explored, and camped.

When our children—Ben, Malindi, Polly and Luke—were small, we ranged across the state as I had with my parents, hunting and fishing and camping and exploring—in that order. But as they grew up, we grew away from hunting and fishing. Our trips to Oregon's wild places gradually focused more on seeing and enjoying and understanding than on what meat we might bring home.

This new focus led me to a whole world of history, myth and legend—components that lend to a place meaning far more profound than that of its physical dimensions alone. It gradually occurred to me that time may be nothing more than a layering of days and years and events, and that short circuits—perhaps aided, as in theatre, by a willing suspension of disbelief —can occur between the layers, making it possible to run with a stone-age hunter along an ancient lakeshore, walk the Meek Cut-off with the 1845 wagon train, or see Coyote and Wishpoosh in their terrible battle when they carved the Columbia Gorge.

For example, in 1856 Indians rolled big rocks down a steep hillside onto soldiers camped near Brushy Bar Riffle on the Rogue River. Terrified, the soldiers dived into their boats and the river carried them away. Last summer I sat on one of those big rocks near Brushy Bar Riffle, ate my dinner, and watched daylight die in the canyon. The river crackles there, rolling rocks along, like summer rain on leafy trees, like a million marbles jostling in a bag. A little blacktail doe browsed behind me, quite unafraid. As I drank my tea, a couple of bears snuffled along the opposite shore. The sky filled with bats as it grew dark and the bears wandered back into the forest. Then, in the indirect moonlight, every rock and bush became a bear or a deer—or an Indian, or a terrified soldier washed up on the riverbank. The night was alive with spirits and I had the essence of Brushy Bar Riffle. For those few moments I had nearly tracked down Coyote.

The Blue Goose is a 1965, 42-passenger, blue Chevrolet school bus, and was once the official Coyote Research Vehicle for Rainy Day Press.

Everything in this book is true. Some of the names have been changed to protect the guilty.

Striking Memories

It was April when the teachers' strike rolled into Eugene that year. My colleagues—the realistic ones—saw it coming, like a freight train down the track of the school year. They thought from early fall that a strike was inevitable, but I continued, right up until the morning it began, to believe that it would not happen. We had, after all, the most pro-teacher and pro-education school board Eugene had had in many years. We had a new tax base and our school district had, for the previous two or three years, been spared the annual embarrassment of going to the polls to ask for more money. We had a superintendent who loved teachers and who believed deeply in the importance of our vocation. Ours, she said, was the most important job in the world, because it makes all the other jobs possible. We looked to her for leadership, friendship, inspiration.

Our school board and our superintendent dropped the responsibility for negotiating the new contract into the lap of a hired-gun negotiator. He bargained by refusing to bargain, and his primary interest, through 15 months of stalling, was his $75-an-hour salary. The school board and superintendent refused to intervene, preferring, instead, to mouth platitudes about "the system", which they saw as "working", though it was clearly not working. The negotiator got rich. We went on strike.

The strike began on Wednesday, April 8, and each day during the first week I thought it would be over the next. I joined my colleagues "on the line", and walked in circles around South Eugene High School. Suddenly the first week was gone. A whole week and all

8

I'd done was carry a sign around an empty building. Picketing seemed a futile and silly enterprise. The strike, it seemed, would end when it ended, with or without my help.

It was clearly time for me to move on, so I did, first alone, to the Clatsop Plains, just west of Astoria, where Coyote met the people. Later, with my 10-year-old son, Luke, and my 14-year-old daughter, Polly, I went to the desert. We circled Steens Mountain that week, camping and climbing and exploring and swimming—tracking down Coyote.

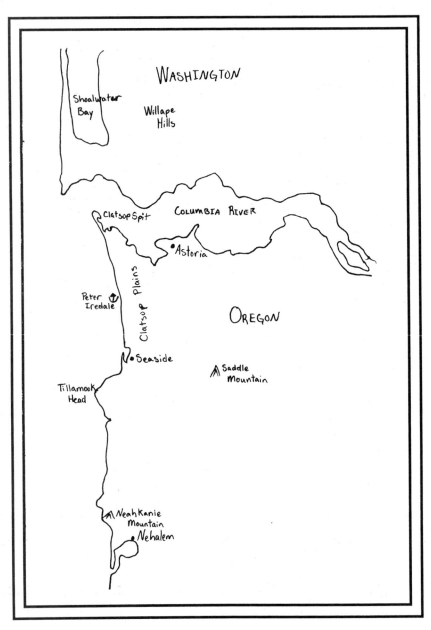

Oregon's Northwest Corner

The Northwest Corner

For the first time I felt I was getting close to the West of my deepest imaginings—the place where the tangible and the mythical become the same.

Edward Abbey
The Journey Home

First, Coyote made the great river. Then he invented the tribes.

In those days, of course, the earth was flat. Gullied here and there by creeks and rivers, it floated like a biscuit in an incomprehensible and intemperate sea. Not much was known about the edge of the world, but it was plain to see from the shore and from the narrow band of water just beyond the breakers that there was an edge, or an end to the water that constantly assaulted the beach and that the end was just over the horizon where the walls of the sky rose and soared round overhead like the inside of an inverted bowl...

I've dreamed this very scene a dozen times. I'm sitting in the Blue Goose, writing. Gulls wheel and squeal overhead and the wind gently rocks the old bus, bending the dune grass toward the east. I'm facing north and through the front window of the bus I can see (or could see, a minute ago—a fogbank rolled in over there and obscured my view) the lighthouse across the Columbia River in Washington. To my right, on the river, an orange and tan ship with cargo booms like angled masts glides upriver toward Astoria and Portland. I can't see the water from here, so the ship slides through the dune grass, reminding me of photographs of oil tankers on the Suez Canal taken so they appear to proceed through the desert sand. I can't see the ocean from here, either, but I can hear it throwing itself at the jetty, roaring above the wind.

This is Clatsop Spit, Oregon's northwestern-most point. About 300 yards from here the spit ends and the Columbia and the Pacific are separated for another half mile or so by the south jetty. Coyote and the others who lived here long ago—when the animals were people who walked and talked as we do today—left much evidence of their passing. This northwest corner of Oregon is sacred territory and when you walk here you walk on hallowed ground. Consider:

A great while ago, in the wonderful age of the ancients, when all kinds of animals spoke and reasoned, and before the present race of Indians existed, there was a mighty beaver, Wishpoosh, that lived in Lake Cleellum. This beaver was god of the lake, owning it, and claiming property in all the fish, wood, and everything in and about its waters. He lived in the bottom of the lake. His eyes were like living fire, his eyebrows bright red, and his immense claws shone and glistened like burnished silver.

He had made the lake and its surroundings a place of terror, for he destroyed and devoured every living thing that came his way. To those he could not kill, he denied the privilege of taking fish, of which there were plenty in the water. All about in the country the people were hungry for fish, and, with plenty nearby, it seemed hard that they must starve.

Coyote, in his journeyings, found the people in this sad plight, and their condition moved him to do something for their relief. As many unsuccessful attempts had been made to destroy the monster, Coyote knew he had a big job on hand, and so made elaborate preparations for the encounter. He armed himself with a powerful spear with a long and strong handle. This spear he bound to his wrist with strong cords of twisted ta-hoosh (Indian flax). Thus equipped he went up to the lake and, finding old Wishpoosh there, drove his spear into him.

The wounded and enraged water god plunged out into the lake and down to the bottom. The cord of the spear handle being fast to Coyote's wrist, he was dragged along by the infuriated beast, so that now the two went plunging and tearing along through the lake. A fearful struggle ensued, in which they tore a gap through the mountain, and came wallowing and swimming into the lake that then covered Kittitass Valley. On across that they came and crashed through the ridge forming the Nahchess Gap, and entered the lake that then stood over the Yakima Valley. Still the mighty beaver god struggled, and Coyote hung on, and they struck the ridge below the Ahtanum, and tore through, forming Union Gap. They went floundering on down, tearing the channel of the Yakima River.

Poor Coyote was getting badly worsted, and was almost strangled, and was clutching at trees along the bank, trying to stop his wild career down the stream. He caught hold of the large cottonwoods, but they broke off or pulled up. He tried the firs; but they tore out by the roots. He clawed at the rocks, but they crumbled off. Nothing could stand before the irresistible power of the mighty Wishpoosh.

Exhausted and almost drowned, he found himself wallowing in the mouth of the Columbia among the breakers. The muskrat was standing on the shore, laughing at him. By this time, the beaver god was dead, and now, half drowned, Coyote came out, dragging his game with him.

He wiped the water from his face and eyes and proceeded to cut up the beaver's carcass. As he cut the different parts, he made of them the Indian tribes. Of the belly he made the lower Columbia and the coast Indians, saying, "You shall always be short and fat, and have great bellies." Of the legs he made the Cayuses, saying, "You shall be fleet of foot and strong of limb." Of the head he made the northern tribes, saying, "You will be men of brains, and strong in war." Of the ribs he made the Yakimas or Pshwan-wa-pams. The various tribes had characteristics derived from the parts from which they were taken. Last of all there was a lot of blood, pieces of entrails and filth, *which Coyote gathered up and flung off toward the country of the Sioux and Snakes, saying, "You shall always be people of blood and violence."*[1]

With one calamitous fight, Coyote created the Columbia River and peopled the land. And when he stopped and looked around after he dragged the carcass of Wishpoosh ashore and distributed it, he stood right here, on Clatsop Spit.

In those days Clatsop Plains, the hundred or so square miles of sandy plains that stretch from here to Tillamook Head, did not exist. Coyote liked to run along the edge of the water but along here there was no beach and the breakers drove him right up into the forest where spruce and pine needles stuck into his nose and made him sneeze. This made him angry, of course, so he stopped and scooped up some sand and threw it at the ocean, saying, "The sea shall go away from here; grass shall grow and people dwell here." Thus Coyote built Clatsop Plains.[2]

The wind picked up and the fogbank that obscured my view of Washington a few minutes ago rolls wet across the grass. The bus rocks and rain splatters against its windward side. Somewhere high up a gull shits in the wind and that, too, splatters on the window at my side. Below me, in a swampy lowland, one lonely mallard drake wanders about, lost among hundreds of white gulls hunkered down behind the jetty to wait out the storm.

Just over there, on the beach, Coyote found the people. He'd heard they were in big trouble, held captive by an evil witch or sorceress, and he came along to help them out:

The journeyings of Coyote began at the ocean, at the mouth of the Columbia River, where lived an atatahlia, an evil creature who was constantly destroying people by tying them upon a baby board and sending them adrift into the foggy distance with the command, "Go forever!" After a time the board came floating back to her, and upon it there was nothing but bones, for on its voyage it had been to

14

a place of such intense heat that the flesh was melted away. On the shore sat many people awaiting their turn to be set adrift. Their hearts would have run away, but the power of the atatahlia held them there.

Then Coyote came among them, and after watching the evil one for a time, he told them, "I will try that, and soon I will return."

So he was tied to the board, and, as he started to drift out into the fog, the old woman said, "Go forever!" But all the people cried out, "Come back again!"

After a while the watchers could faintly see the board drifting closer, and they wondered if Coyote had been powerful enough to survive; and when it touched the shore they saw that he was alive, and all the people were glad.

Then, to prove which was the stronger, the woman was placed on the board and went out into the fog, while Coyote and all the people shouted, "Go forever!" In time the board came drifting back with nothing but her bleached bones upon it.

The people were happy that the evil was destroyed and urged their deliverer to take from their number a wife. But he said: "No, I do not want a wife. I am to travel up the river."[3]

Coyote saw that the people he had freed were a helpless lot, and he knew he would have to do all he could to help them out. By then, all the fish in the world were owned by two sisters who lived upriver...

Coming near to the place, he saw the two women in their canoe catching driftwood. Wishing to get into their place, he formed himself into a piece of alder, slipped into the water, and floated down. As he passed close to the canoe, the younger woman cried, "See that nice piece of alder!"

But the other one did not wish to secure it. "Here are smaller ones," she said; "let that one go."

After passing out of sight, Coyote floated ashore and returned to the point from which he had started. Having studied the matter for a while, he became a piece of cedar, thinking that perhaps they would take that kind of wood, which they could use in making their drying racks. Again he drifted close to the boat, and the younger sister called attention to the cedar log, but the elder did not seem to wish it.

The next time he formed himself into a piece of oak, but this, too, the elder woman rejected. A long fir pole was Coyote's next disguise, but even this, which would have been so useful to lay from eave to eave and hang dried fish on, did not appeal to the elder sister, and was allowed to float by.

Coyote's ingenuity was almost exhausted and for a long time he sat on the bank meditating before he transformed himself into a little baby, strapped to a board. He floated down the river toward the women, crying lustily. Water began to lap into his mouth, and it seemed to him that he must soon choke, when the younger woman cried excitedly: "Here is a baby! Someone has tipped over and lost it. Quick, let us get it."

The elder said, "No, sister, we do not need a baby," and began to paddle away; but the other seized her own paddle and endeavored to force the canoe toward the drowning infant. They paddled with all their might, and the water fairly boiled with the rapid strokes, but, both being of the same strength, neither could make headway, and all the while the baby was drifting nearer to them. At last it came close to the stern, and the younger woman reached out and took it into the canoe. "It is a boy!" she cried. "Now if we rear it we will have someone to help us." So it was agreed that they take the child and care for it.

When they reached home they untied the child and removed it from its wrappings. The younger said to herself: "What are we going to feed this baby? I will give it a piece of dried lamprey to suck." She did so, and the baby eagerly took the lamprey, which was soon eaten.

She laced it up on its board, cut off another piece, and when this was about half eaten, the baby fell asleep. "Now the baby is sleeping, we can go and get more wood," said she.

The elder woman was uneasy since the coming of the infant. She took no interest in it, and did not wish to help care for it. The two went out and began to catch driftwood.

When Coyote found it quiet in the house, he opened his eyes. Quickly he unlaced his cover, crept slyly out, and saw the women on the river. Inside he found a great abundance of dried lampreys and *other fish, and he hurriedly roasted a quantity on sticks, ate them, and hid the sticks. Then he laced himself to the board, put the half-eaten piece of lamprey in his mouth, and closed his eyes. The women returned and were surprised to find the baby still sleeping. When they retired for the night, the younger sister laid the baby at her side, and Coyote liked that place to sleep, but was all the time thinking how he could let the salmon escape.*

The next morning the younger sister gave him another piece of fish, and, after seeing the child asleep, the two went to the river for wood. Again Coyote crawled out and ate, and then went to the pond in which the fish were impounded. After making five oak root-diggers, he concealed them and returned to the baby board.

The third day Coyote cooked and ate, then took one of his root-diggers, thrust it into the bank of the river, and pried off a great mass of earth. Again and again he repeated this until the digger was blunt and broken, and then he took a new one. This, and a third, and a fourth were used, when the sisters, happening to look up, saw what was going on. As Coyote began to use his fifth digger they started to paddle ashore in great haste, the elder sister saying over and over: "You see, I did not want to take that baby. It was Coyote and we shall lose our fish, and now we shall never live as well as we have lived."

Just as the canoe grounded and they leaped out, Coyote pried off the last mass of earth, and the water began to rush out of the lake, carrying the salmon with it. He picked up a lump of white clay and ran toward the two sisters. "It is not right for you to have all these fish penned up in one place," he cried. "Things are going to change. There will be other beings here besides you."[4]

The people of some tribes believe Coyote changed the sisters to sandpipers, some believe they were changed to swallows. Perhaps both are correct, and that is why swallows swoop and dive over Oregon's rivers today while sandpipers mince and peck along riverbanks and beaches.

Coyote ordered the great fishes, like the whales, to go down the river and live in the sea, and he told the smaller fishes, like the salmon, to go upstream and populate the river and its tributaries. Then he formed a partnership with the lizard and the bat right here at the mouth of the Columbia to catch salmon for himself and for the people to eat. At first, because he offended the salmon, he did not do well. But Sahalee Tyee, the chief above, taught him etiquette. Coyote learned fast:

> *They (Coyote, Lizard and Bat) made a net by splitting the roots of the spruce and tying the strands together. They then tied pieces of driftwood to the top of the net and stones to its lower edge, and Coyote paddled out with one end of the net and set it in a curve and came ashore with his end. Then they hauled the net in, and caught only one salmon. Coyote was angry because of their ill luck and asked the great Spirit for a reason. "Any fool ought to know he must fish for salmon on the ebb tide," was the answer.*
>
> *"It is enough. I have heard," said Coyote.*
>
> *Next day they caught two. Again Coyote protested. He was told that the day before they had tramped upon the salmon. That salmon must always be kept clean, else they would be ashamed, and not come to the river.*
>
> *Three the next day, and again Coyote asks: "What's the matter now?"*
>
> *"Yesterday you cut the salmon in blocks. Never do that. Cut down the backbone and open the fish that way."*
>
> *A little better luck—four—the next day. Then they learned that cooking three salmon, when unable to eat half of one, would make the salmon ashamed, and they would refuse to enter the river.*
>
> *Thus, day after day, they were given all the precepts of the salmon tabu, which to this day is observed by the Indians on many rivers north of the Columbia.*[5]

The rain's hard now, the wind driving it in horizontally from the southwest. Though it's spring on the calendar, it still looks like winter here, a perfect Oregon coast sort of day, the kind of day when you can almost be assured of having the beach to yourself.

To my left is an observation platform, built on a base of

four large poles—like power poles—driven into the sand behind the jetty. The platform, about 20 feet square, is about 15 feet above the ground, just over the height of the jetty. The remains of a little railroad, apparently built to transport huge rocks that form the jetty from an inland quarry, stretches from here across the Clatsop Plains and on across the shallow water to the mainland. The rails are gone but much of the wooden trestle remains.

On a clear day the wreck of the *Peter Iredale*, a British schooner that ran aground just south of here in October, 1906, and Tillamook Head, ten or 12 miles to the south, are visible from the tower, but today visibility is limited to a few hundred yards. I climbed over the jetty and headed south along the beach, looking for the *Peter Iredale*.

By-the-wind sailors die by the millions along the coast every spring. Round and gray like little jellyfish, they float along on the ocean's surface, but they are cursed with an extra little flap that projects into the wind like a sail. If the wind blows to the shore, that's where they must go. Slippery, smelly, and dirty-looking in their annual mass-death, they pile up along the beaches. Yesterday I saw piles of them on the lee side of the jetty, borne over the top by high waves and hard wind.

I leaned into the wind, watching gulls and sandpipers as they waited expectantly for the ocean to bring their dinner. They weren't disappointed and I wasn't either.

Along the beach I found the usual array of whiskey and gin bottles, some large brown bottles with Japanese writing on them, elegant clear glass bottles with no writing on them, two little glass floats from Japan, eight or ten plastic floats shaped like razor clams, one small and one large (with a diameter of about ten inches) round plastic float, a fish box with Japanese writing on it, and a sturdy red plastic crate that was probably used for transporting Japanese soft drink or beer bottles.

I stopped to watch a gull try to crack open a razor clam. He picked it off the beach, flew to 20 or 25 feet above the beach and dropped it. The clam bounced, the gull pounced, pecked and picked it up again. Bounce, pounce, peck. Bounce, pounce, peck. Again and again the gull dropped the clam, but the thing would not crack. I counted 22 attempts made by the persistent gull, but still he could not get inside the clam. After a while I moved close enough to see the problem. The gull was trying to open a float. Three times I saw gulls bouncing clam-shaped plastic floats off the beach.

Visibility was so limited that for quite a long period during my hike I could see neither my destination, the *Peter Iredale*, nor my point of origin, the jetty. As I walked along in the rain I thought of Coyote's people imprisoned on this stretch of beach and began to fantasize about walking right by the Peter Iredale and on toward California. I was alone in a little time capsule, or weather capsule, and what if, I thought, I was the only person on earth. I might be, for all the evidence I could see—that is, until I saw the pickup. A rusty old Chevrolet, it materialized out of the fog in front of me, heading slowly north toward the jetty. The closer it got, the slower it went. As it passed, the driver scrutinized me impassively, like a scientist watching an organism through a microscope. The pickup went on up the beach about 100 yards, turned, and came back, even slower. I could clearly see the driver—a mean, unshaven face, beady eyes fixed on me, greasy baseball cap pulled over his prominent brow. Slower and slower he came, and closer, peering through the rain, apparently not wanting to miss a detail.

"People disappear along here," I thought. I was alone, unarmed. No one else knew where I was. I formulated a variety of escape strategies as he drove to within five feet of me, slowed to my walking pace and watched me through the passenger side window. Then, as suddenly as he had appeared out of the fog, he was gone back into it. Only his tracks in the sand and the hammering of my heart evidenced his passing.

Alone in the fog, I again contemplated Coyote's wonderful world:

The large rocks off Tillamook Head, at the south end of

Clatsop Plains, where Tillamook Lighthouse is now, were once a man and a woman and their children. They disobeyed Coyote (They knew him by his Chinook name, Talipus.) by trying to walk on the water. He changed them to stone.

A wizard and his brother once came among the Clatsops from somewhere in the north. They claimed to have beneficial magic, but they brought, instead, head lice. When Coyote heard of their gift he turned them to stone and they, too, still stand in the surf near Tillamook Head.

Coyote wasn't the only legend in the neighborhood, though. One day, before white men appeared in Oregon (about 1679, according to one source[6]; 1745, according to another[7]), three sailing ships, unlike anything ever seen along this coast, appeared on the horizon about ten miles south of here. The Indians likened the ships to big canoes, their sails like wings, and said that they "boomed" at one another. In another version, "poof, poof," was the sound that they made as they fought beyond the breakers. Two of the ships eventually sank. The third, badly damaged, made a run for the beach at the bottom of Neahkahnie Mountain, where it broke up in the surf, strewing the beach with wreckage, including a large amount of beeswax, blocks of which have been exposed occasionally by the tide even in recent times. Twenty-eight sailors, including one giant black man, stumbled ashore from the wreck, burdened with whatever essentials they could carry and a large chest, which they dragged up the mountainside and buried. In one version of the legend, the black man was killed and buried with the chest, his spirit to protect it forever.

To the Indians, who until then assumed that there was only one race, these men of different colors must have been a terrifying sight, but, as was their custom, they welcomed the strangers to their village, offered food, and helped the men to obtain shelter for the coming winter. As was their custom, the white men took food, land, and other belongings from the Indians and, in return, offered venereal disease, measles, and violence.

During the third year after the arrival of the white men, a council was held between the Clatsops, the Tillamooks and the Nehalems. They had had enough. Before dawn one autumn morning, 1500 warriors crept into the camp of the white men, set fire to their dwellings and killed them all as they ran from the flames. The Indians buried the men on the mountain near where the black man and the box were buried. After this massacre, the river ran red with blood for three days.

Other evidence points to the presence of a treasure on Neahkahnie Mountain. Records exist of Spanish treasure ships that sailed north from Peru and disappeared. Rocks with mysterious markings, clues, perhaps, to the location of the treasure, were found at the base of the mountain, others somewhat higher up the mountain. Stone walls, masonry and giant mounds of rocks placed in the shape of an inverted "W" with a base nearly a mile long have been discovered by treasure hunters near Neahkahnie.

Neahkahnie has attracted a regular army of treasure hunters over the years, including five who died in the course of their search, and one who called me one afternoon last winter.

The caller, who asked that I not use his name, said he had spent 20 years digging around Neahkahnie Mountain and that he had a story like a Stephen King book about the things that had happened to him during that time.

He said he'd found and crawled through 1632 feet of tunnels lined with cedar planks. The tunnels led to a star shaped chamber and, while he was in the chamber, three-dimensional demons appeared before him, voices spoke to him, and other apparitions appeared to him. Blood appeared on his back, on his pillow case, and on his Bible, sometimes in the shape of a triangle, sometimes in the shape of a cross. When a demon appeared to him down in the tunnels he held out his Bible and said, "I renounce you in the name of Jesus." The demon disappeared.

Once, when he was down in the tunnels, his wife saw a ball of fire appear out of the ocean, turn into a man, and walk down the beach.

He has deciphered the treasure rocks: the Ws stand for tunnels, the dots for treasure chambers. The gold ingots are buried on the beach; jewels on the mountainside. The secret to the mountainside treasure is on a concrete capstone buried with the gold ingots on the beach.

"This treasure thing," he said, "is like the Bible and the Arc of the Covenant. It's meant for one man to decipher and one man to find. It's between the Devil and God." He spoke with the devil inside the mountain. Two people, he told me, were driven crazy on the mountain.

"The old sailors navigated by the stars," he said, at last. "How would you bury it?"

Last spring, my head full of pirates and treasure, I went to Neahkahnie. I poked around on the beach beneath the mountain, trying, as all those treasure hunters before me, to figure the most likely spot that the chest could be buried. Then I climbed the mountain and stood for a while at the top, looking south past Tillamook and west across the ocean. Clearcuts, of course, were the dominant feature of the forest to the north and east, as they are in all Oregon's forests these days, but it wasn't hard to imagine what it must have looked like the day the birdlike canoes sailed across the horizon and fought beyond the breakers.

The mountain is steep, rising abruptly from the beach 1631 feet to its crest, which was a little south of where I thought it would be. If I were burying the treasure I'd not want to drag it very far up the precipitous face of the mountain. I'd want it high enough to be safe from the surf, but low enough so that I could retrieve it readily when I returned. My guess is that, if there is a treasure, it's buried on the west flank of the mountain in a spot visible from the ocean, just high enough to be safe from the highest tides.

Just north of here, across the Columbia River, Cheatco chased Tsmtsmts and his four brothers around Shoalwater Bay. From that race rose the hills along the north shore at the mouth of the Columbia. We still hear Cheatco, of course. I can hear him as I walk. He was sentenced by Old Thunder to forecast the weather.

Long ago, when the animals were still gigantic in size and shape, and talked like human beings, and men were few, there lived five brothers on the east side of Shoalwater Bay. The name of the youngest was Tsmtsmts. He was small for his age, and while the other brothers went hunting all the time and had great enjoyment, he was compelled to stay at home and work from morning until night.

It was his task to make the bows and arrows that the others used for shooting game, to gather the roots and steam them and ravel them into threads and twist the twines with which his brothers caught fish; and to take care of the young dogs that would be used by the brothers for tracking the wild animals. He probably also had to dress the skins brought in by the hunters and used as covers at night. In short, his work was much like that put upon the Indian women; but as there seems to have been no woman in this family it was imposed upon Tsmtsmts, because he was the youngest and smallest.

He grew very tired of his tasks, but he also became skillful and shrewd. He felt so lonesome when the rest were gone that he made up many songs and sang constantly as he worked, or as he went into the woods to gather roots or while he was weaving twines. In some of his songs he had a refrain, "Come here, come here," and this sounded through the woods and he felt as if people were talking with him. But his brothers said, when they came home and heard him singing, "Stop calling on someone to come here; the Cheatco will hear you and really come. He will eat us all up."

The Cheatco was a giant who roamed the woods and had a terrible staff, with which he would sometimes strike down the old dry stubs in the forest. Tsmtsmts would keep still, until his brothers were gone and then sing and call, "Come here," louder than ever. He was so lonesome that he would rather see the giant than no one.

As the brothers predicted, the Cheatco came. He had probably heard Tsmtsmts singing. His appearance was more terrible than it had been described. He was of monstrous size; he carried a great staff made of dead men's bones and in his teeth were clinging the locks of hair of his victims recently eaten.

It was advisable to treat such a guest with great courtesy. He was invited into the house, several of the largest boards being taken down from the side of the house to let him in. He was given the best place before the fire, which was brightened up, and the best food in the house was given him to eat. The older brothers behaved with great decorum; but Tsmtsmts, being small, acted the part of the saucy boy.

"What are you going to eat, Giant?" he asked.

"I will eat these fine trout and this fine venison," he answered.

"What will you eat then?"

"I will eat your blankets"—that is, the skins used for bedcovers.

"Then what will you eat?"

"I will eat you," responded the Cheatco, grinding his teeth.

Tsmtsmts laughed and cried out: "Shut your mouth, Giant."

When it came bed time, the Cheatco demanded that someone come with him, and Tsmtsmts readily volunteered. He continued his saucy talk and at intervals would shout out: "Keep your mouth shut, Giant," but contrived to tell his brothers that he would watch, and they must go to bed as usual next to the wall, but be ready to creep out under the roof and run away when they heard him shout.

Sometime in the night the Cheatco woke and feeling hungry, determined to eat the brothers. Tsmtsmts, who pretended to be asleep but was really carefully observing the giant, now, as if half walking and continuing his antics, cried out as heretofore, "Keep your mouth shut, Giant"—and, at the warning, the four brothers hastily slipped through the wall where they had prepared an opening and took the well known track southward around the head of the bay.

The Cheatco made his spring to catch them, but found only empty couches, and in his rage, seeing the openings where the brothers had escaped, rushed out to pursue them. Tsmtsmts took advantage of the moment and caught up the two young dogs and the skein of twine that he had been twisting and followed his brothers as a sort of rear guard; for when it came to a matter of cunning, he was the best.

In the course of time the Cheatco found their track, and in the *early morning was seen following them. The four brothers were now far ahead, being strong and swift and having no load; they had doubled the head of the bay and were now running northward up the beach for the mouth. Their object was to cross here, if they could, by the grace of the Ferryman, Old Thunder, and thus escape the woods monster, the Cheatco.*

Tsmtsmts, however, was far behind, laboring along with the two young dogs and his big skein of twine. In no great length of time it seemed he must be overtaken; the Cheatco was approaching with huge strides, his mouth open and the hair of former victims still dangling from his teeth. At the proper moment, however, the wily Tsmtsmts paused, threw down the larger of the two dogs and cried out: "Rise up, my earth."

As soon as the dog actually touched the ground the earth rose, making some lofty hills immediately in front of the giant, which rise to this day in the shape of a dog and from a range known to the Indians as the Solee hills. By this sudden intervention of the earth, the Cheatco, huge as he was, was thrown backwards, and tumbled many a time before being able to cross the obstruction. This he did, however, and in course of time was following and approaching Tsmtsmts.

When he came too near, the boy paused, threw down his remaining dog, the smaller one, and said: "Rise up, my earth," and another, but lower range of hills rose up, tumbling the monster back once more. This formed a second range of hills, dog-shaped, of which the western end forms the cape now known as North Head, at the mouth of the Columbia. On the outer rocks of this cape the waves still rise and fall, much in the way that the giant rose and fell back trying to cross the obstruction that the earth heaved up.

But he succeeded, and along in the afternoon was seen approaching. The brothers had long since reached the mouth of the bay—Shoalwater—where it unites with the ocean. They had been hailing Old Thunder (the ancient ferryman) on the other side, imploring him by all the moving terms they knew to take them over. They would call, "Oh, Grandfather, take us over," but he would say gruffly, "I have no grandchildren."

Then they would say, "Oh, Uncle, take us over," but he would answer, "I have no nephews," and continue with his work. He was making nets to catch whales in the ocean.

When at length Tsmtsmts arrived, he was followed very closely by the Cheatco, who now felt sure of his prey, and, as might be expected, after running all day and contending with the earth which threw mountains in his way, was very hungry. The brothers were in great terror, and now implored Old Thunder more loudly than ever, calling him grandfather and uncle—but got no answer.

But Tsmtsmts, jumping upon the shore held aloft his skein of twine and said, "Take us across, Thunder, and I will give you this." Old Thunder just happened to be needing twine to finish his nets, and readily agreed to take them. His manner of ferrying was peculiar—it was simply to extend his leg across the water and upon this, as a footlog, the passengers might go. The five brothers lost no time in running across the leg and putting the inlet between themselves and the Cheatco.

They were scarcely safely landed on the north side, however, before the Cheatco reached the opposite shore. He called to Thunder to put out his leg and take him over also, as he was a friend of the young men. This Thunder agreed to do, but looked with much suspicion at the staff, made of dead men's bones. "You must not touch me with that," he said, and stretched out his leg. The Cheatco began walking upon this ancient ferriage, but arriving at the middle of the water and looking down and seeing the tide swirling out he felt dizzy and inadvertently thrust down his staff to steady himself. At that instant the leg was withdrawn, the man-eating monster was dumped headlong into the tide and carried out far to sea.

Old Thunder then called out in his great voice, "Oh wicked Cheatco! Long enough have you been roaming the earth and devouring men. Now you shall be of use to them. You shall no longer live in the woods, but in the sea, and when there is to be a storm you must go far south and roar for the storm, to let people know that it is coming. When the storm is near, you must come up near and roar and show that it is about passing by. When the weather is to be fair, you must go north and roar for fair weather."

This destiny the Cheatco has fulfilled ever since. He goes far *south and roars, sometimes two days beforehand, for a storm; when the storm is about to pass, he comes up near and roars. When it is to be fair, he goes north and roars.*[8]

Hoolee[9], the south wind, drives the rain across the beach and I can hear the old Cheatco now, roaring out of the southwest, though the storm is already upon me. My windward side is soaked, the lee, nearly dry.

Long ago, the thunderbird daily searched the ocean for whales, which he snatched from the water in his enormous talons and brought to the top of Saddle Mountain, just a few miles southeast of here. He was seen only by a few special medicine men, and they told how thunder boomed from his enormous wings and lightning bolts shot from his eyes. The first men were hatched from thunderbird eggs at the base of Saddle Mountain. Later, when the Clatsop Indians lived here, young men came to the mountain, which they called Swallalahost[10], seeking their Tamanahwous, or guardian spirits.

My son, Luke, and I climbed that mountain one summer afternoon and sat for a time at the top, sharing a peach and some chocolate. Wind whistled round the rocks. A vaporous wraith, fog, swirled up the western side, obscured the sun and the surrounding hills, isolating us on the barren peak. In our minds' eye we saw Thunderbird, perched there with us like an eagle on a fencepost, a whale in his fist, eating it as calmly as we ate the peach. A young Indian, filled with the reality of Thunderbird, rose up out of the fog, out of the past. He carried no weapon, no food. For days he had eaten only roots and berries. Weak, hungry, expectant, he approached. He had been traveling for days from his village. He was told to bathe in each stream, to avoid trails and men. He knew that a vision awaited, an apparition unmistakably his and his alone. Out there in that vast wilderness, somewhere on the mountain, his tamahnahwous waited. Then laughter rode in out of the fog, from the north, banishing Thunderbird, the young Indian, and the past. Two hikers, young men in Bermuda shorts appeared over the ledge. Luke and I hiked back to the Blue Goose.

But today it's the *Peter Iredale* I seek, and soon I find it. The old ship looks much diminished from my previous visits as it emerges from the mist in the distance. For more than 80 years it withstood the worst the Pacific could throw at it, but the last few years have taken large toll on the old ship. It is smaller, less imposing this time. Two fishermen, tough old men oblivious to the icy conditions, stand hip-deep in the waves just beyond the rusty steel skeleton, casting with long, stout poles into the surf. The Chevrolet pickup pauses where the beach meets the road and then disappears inland and I am alone with the *Peter Iredale*.

I place my hand on the ship's rusty side and hear my mother's voice. "Be careful", the universal call of parents everywhere. There's our old blue Buick at the road's end, my sisters and I clambering through the jagged, rusty guts of the old wreck. My parents stand on the beach, anxiously calculating the surf, fearful that a sneaker wave will roar out of nowhere and snatch their children, but willing, too, that we should make a few judgments of our own. "Be careful." I hear it again, but this time it's my own voice and those are my little children clambering on the old rustpile. My wife, Chris, and I stand on the beach, calculating the tide, watching for sneaker waves, worried, but hesitant to call them back.

"Got a light?" The Chevrolet pickup is back. The driver stands beside me in a green rubber tent of rain gear, carrying a plastic bucket, half full of bait, and a long surf pole.

"Yeah." Startled, I fish around in my pockets and find a soggy book of matches. The matchheads dissolve when I try to strike them. "Sorry."

"Oughta quit anyway," he grunts and trudges into the surf.

I trudge north, the wind driving the rain into my dry side now. In just a few yards I'm soaked on both sides, my boots full of water. The weather closes around me and I am again alone on the beach.

Soon, the rain lets up and in the distance I can see the jetty and the observation tower. My pockets are full of rainwater and plastic, clam-shaped floats, and I am as wet as if I had walked the whole way in the surf. The Cheatco still howls as Hoolee drives the surf over the end of the jetty. A pink plastic float, as big as a basketball and much heavier, dangles from a barnacle-encrusted rope thrown over my shoulder. The red plastic beer bottle box, white Japanese characters legible beneath a little crop of seaweed, furrows the sand at my side. Two little glass floats from Japan are safely tucked inside the box.

Later, inside the Blue Goose once again, rain still drumming on the roof, I peel off layer after layer of soaked clothing and spread it over the bunks to drip. The old bus rocks in the wind as night arrives and, above the storm, I hear Old Man Coyote, riding the wind and making waves, just as he did in the beginning. With his mad song in my ear, I drift off to sleep.

April in the Desert

Once Coyote fell in love with Evening Star. Each night he climbed to the top of the highest peak to try to speak with her. At first she ignored him, but he persisted and, at last, she could ignore him no more.

"There is no place for you in the heavens," she told him, "but I'll fly low tomorrow night and speak with you if you will agree never to bother me again."

Coyote agreed immediately. The next night found him high on a mountain peak, waiting for Evening Star to come out and speak with him. When at last darkness came, she rode low in the sky. As she began to speak, Coyote jumped up and grabbed her with his paws. Terrified, she fled into the heavens.

Coyote was overjoyed. He danced through the heavens with Evening Star in his arms. Evening Star, still terrified, fled higher and higher into the sky and Coyote became unbearably cold. At last he was too cold to hang on and Evening Star slipped from his grasp.

Coyote fell through space for a very long time. When he finally crashed to earth he was smashed flat and permanently weakened by the impact. Since that time he's never been able to jump into the heavens again, but Coyote can still be seen and heard at night howling his love for Evening Star.[1]

Monday:

The Blue Goose charged up the McKenzie River Valley to the top of the Cascades. On the east side, just past Sisters, a coyote grinned at us from a roadside field—wishing us luck on

31

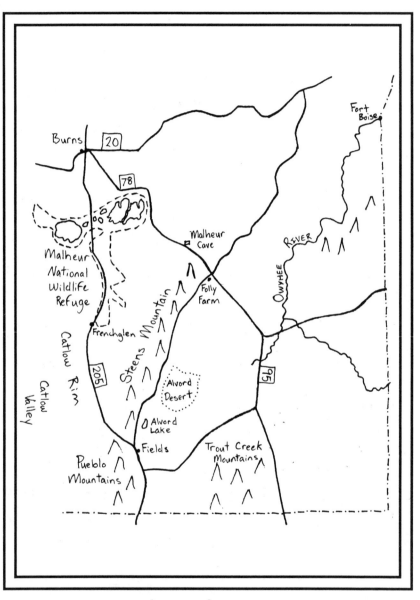

Oregon's Southeastern Corner

our journey—and then loped on. He stopped occasionally and turned toward us, tongue hanging out in the mid-day heat, and then, as if to say, "No more time for you right now, Bub," he was gone.

We rolled on through Bend and out across central Oregon. In December, when we made this same trip, the Blue Goose lost power and ground slowly to a halt in a snowstorm just south of Burns. That time the gas line froze solid—clearly not the problem today—but the Blue Goose had some of the same symptoms on this warm, windy afternoon. We pushed on, though, slowly. The old engine struggling mightily with every little rise in the terrain. In Burns we filled the big tank with gas and checked the engine over. It ran smoothly then, so I hoped that the problem had solved itself and we turned east again, out of town, looking for Malheur Cave.

We were still looking for Malheur Cave when the sun went down. We camped on the shore of a little desert lake at the confluence of Camp Creek and Indian Creek. The south fork of the Malheur River flows north from this little lake. Ducks and geese, yellow-headed blackbirds, red-winged blackbirds and meadowlarks trilled, tweeted, honked, quacked and warbled. We knew from the map and from the directions we'd received in New Princeton that we were close, but we still had not found the cave.

The Water Cave was once the water-imps' country, it was said by our forefathers. Many of them say they saw such creatures in the cave, and they did not lie. You can still see rocks piled up by the water-imps there.[2]

As soon as the bus stopped we dragged our bicycles out and the kids were off across the desert with my caution about cowboys driving 90 miles an hour along these desert roads not expecting to see a couple of kids on bicycles when they come around that corner ringing through the sagebrush after them. Clouds of near-mosquitoes descended on us—just to have a look, I think, because they did not bite—and then went away with the breeze. I got out the stove and cooked up a pot of canned chili, straight from the shelf at the Burns Safeway, for dinner.

Later, in the dark, Polly and Luke and I sat on the edge of the lake, lined up like theater-goers, watching the grand dance of a lightning storm on hilltops miles away. "You know," Luke said, "we never did this before— just sat and watched lightning."

Except for a little breeze sighing in the sagebrush and the occasional rustle of a duck on the water, it was quiet and we discussed the lightning: Why is there no thunder and does lightning strike from the ground up or from the sky down? I'd always thought that lightning came from the sky down, but I didn't know why there was no thunder. I'd seen it strike pine trees in the Blue Mountains and go sizzling round and round the tree from the top down and leave a track like a corkscrew down the trunk, but some of the lightning we watched that night struck from the hilltops to the sky and some didn't strike at all but rolled like a big luminous ball across the horizon.

Back in the days of Coyote's people (the Watteetash), Thunder, who was known in those days as Eenumtla, was a dreadful tyrant. From his perch high in the clouds he saw everything and everyone. With a wink of his terrible eye, he could send a lightning bolt flashing across the sky with terrifying accuracy to strike anyone he chose. When he was in a bad mood, which was most of the time, he would spread dark clouds in the sky above anyone he saw and thunder so violently as to shake the earth all around. Then, in an instant, a lightning bolt would strike and that person would be no more.

Coyote was traveling around down in Oregon one time— maybe he was right out here in the desert—and he found the people depressed and so afraid of being struck by lightning that they would not leave their houses.   "What's going on?" he asked. "Why are you all so afraid?"

They told Coyote of their fear of Eenumtla, of how they could not leave their houses to fish or hunt. Because of this fear, starvation threatened the tribe. "This is not good," said Coyote, and he promised to break the power of the storm god.

Coyote pondered the problem for a long while, but could not think of a way to vanquish Eenumtla, so, as was his custom, he brought forth his sisters from his belly and asked them for advice.

"Why should we tell you?" they asked. "You'll just claim credit for any idea we come up with. We're not going to help you this time."

This angered Coyote, so he threatened to have the snow cover them up. Coyote's sisters hated to be cold, so they quickly thought up a plan. They whispered it into Coyote's ear and he said, "Yes, that is what I thought. That is what I was going to do." Then he put the sisters back into his belly.

Coyote then transformed himself into a feather and began to drift along on the wind. Higher and higher he drifted, until he was in the clouds with Eenumtla, who was puzzled by his appearance. "That looks like a feather," he thought, "yet it looks like Coyote." He pondered the feather, but decided that it was probably only what it appeared to be, a feather that he had blasted off of someone a few days earlier. He raised up and thundered and sent some rain to wash it away. To his great surprise, the feather did not move.

When the rain ceased, the magic feather began to thunder and throw out lightning bolts and great sheets of rain. Eenumtla was sorely perplexed that a feather could put on such a show. "I thought I was the only one who could do that," he said to himself. Determined not to be outdone by such an insignificant little thing as a feather, he conjured up a terrible storm, thundering until the skies shook and pouring down rain upon the frightened earth. In return, Coyote took a deep breath and began to toss lightning bolts right into the eyes of Eenumtla. The thunder god was surprised, but he did not dodge or *blink. He met Coyote's new attack with a new one of his own.*

The battle went on for days. Each volley brought an even fiercer reply, until the sky burned and the earth was flooded. At last, Eenumtla and Coyote crashed together high in the clouds. There they fought, rolling over and over, thunder and lightning and rain blasting forth, until they crashed to earth with so much force that the whole world shook.   Fortunately, when they hit the ground, Coyote was on top and he was able to seize the advantage. His sisters had foreseen just such a situation and had equipped Coyote with five war clubs. Coyote beat the stunned Eenumtla until each of the five war clubs broke, beat him until the old thunder god lay helpless in the dirt, barely able to plead for mercy.

"No longer will it be your habit to kill and terrify people," Coyote told him. *"You can thunder on hot, sultry, days from now on, and you may flash lightning, but not to destroy."*

Eenumtla's power has been broken since that day. He still has the power to terrify, but he uses it sparingly, and he seldom kills.[3]

In the bus, the soft glow of our battery-powered lamps holds the night at bay. We're a booky group: Polly is reading Valley of the Horses; Luke, The Hobbit; and me, Roadside Geology of Oregon. As usual, all the doors and windows are open. The desert air rustles the curtains and the night sounds— a restless duck or goose thrashing the water, the sibilant wind gentle in the sagebrush, crickets greeting the cool night, but, on this night, no coyote singing the moon down—lull us to sleep. The first night on the desert is special, peaceful, far from the fractious cares of picketers and school boards and the wail of nighttime sirens. One by one the lights go out, mine first.

Tuesday:
    Morning walk. Soil too stony for a good hole, so I pull a rock out, like a plug from a bottle and shit in the hole. Replace the rock and no one will ever know. Leave a clean camp, my

dad always said. Those who don't bury their messes should be made to eat them, I always say.

Found a pile of bones, strewn about and gnawed, and an orange plastic ear tag, all that's left of old Number 12.

Breakfast: fig bars, peanut butter and honey sandwich, and an orange.

We are drinking coffee and hot chocolate and writing in our journals when a white diesel pickup pulls up behind the bus.

"Do you have permission to camp here?" He's a kindly-looking man with steely eyes and a white straw hat and a face that's seen much desert weather.

"I didn't know I needed permission."

"What made you think that?"

"Well, I'm usually pretty careful about getting permission," I assure him, "but there was no sign and no fence and I could see where others had driven off the road and stopped here. We were looking for Malheur Cave and I just assumed that we would be on BLM land when we got in the neighborhood."

"This is all deeded land," he said, scrutinizing the bus and walking around to the far side where he sees Polly and Luke sitting at the edge of the lake. When he sees them he seems to soften a little. Probably we are not what he expected when he saw a blue school bus parked in the middle of his sagebrush this morning. "The cave's on deeded land, too."

"Well, we'll leave if you want..."

"No. No. The cave's over there," he points south, "behind that tree." A lone pine tree stands on a knoll just to the south of us, about half a mile away. "You can stay as long as you want. Just clean up and close the gates."

The cave was over there, behind that tree, but it took us most of the morning to find it. While searching, we saw a mule

37

deer doe standing high up on a rimrock, silhouetted against the sky in a pose I thought they reserved for wildlife photographers. An antelope ran ahead of us for a mile or so while he tried to figure out how to get through the fence on the west side of the road. A deer would have jumped over that fence or scrambled under it, but the antelope ran right up to it a dozen or more times, like he intended to jump, but lost his nerve each time. Finally he gave up and trotted up and over the hill on the east side of the road.

We hiked over to the tree I thought the rancher had pointed to, but no cave was visible. Along the way we picked up stone chips—obsidian—that looked out of place in that sandy soil. We found no perfect arrowheads, but many chips that look like partial arrowheads. I imagined Stone Age craftsmen sitting on the shore of a vanished lake, chipping away, seeking the perfect arrowhead. Their mistakes and rejects are still there, a legacy for us to find.

Because Malheur Cave appears on maps of Harney County, I thought the road to the cave would be substantial, a well-traveled road. It isn't. We'd checked out all the alternatives for a three or four mile stretch along the county road when we came to the last one. We'd already driven by it with the thought that "this can't possibly be the road to the cave. It's hardly a road and it doesn't appear to go very far". But it was— an unlikely-looking trail straggling off into the sagebrush in the direction of Camp Creek near the head of the little lake where we spent the night. So we parked the bus again and started down along it on our bicycles. Luke and Polly led the way and I poked along behind.

The little road forked about three quarters of a mile from the county road. The right fork took us to Camp Creek, where we scared up a family of geese who flew off, honking indignantly and soaring away below us as we stood on the cliff that formed the stream bank. What seemed to be the main part of the road went straight ahead, eventually meandering down to a little green meadow along the creek. The meadow narrowed as we went downstream, and the cliffs along the banks grew higher, forming a natural corral that ended where the deep water began at the head of the little lake. An outhouse stood in the meadow, door open, seat up, all shot full of holes. A rectangular shed with a carport-like shelter resting on 4x4 posts stood a little farther down the meadow, nearer the deep water. The shed was filled with weathered-looking lumber.

The left fork finally took us to the cave. Coyote, of course, knew about the cave all along. It was he who told the Indians.

In the days before the coming of the white man, Piute Indians believed in the transmigration of souls to the Coyote and later to heaven, where all were restored to youth and lived forever midst plentiful wild game, flowers, trees, lakes, and streams.

Many, many years ago, long before the white man came to this country, when Malheur Lake was high and flowed out through the old river channel past Malheur Cave and was the headwaters of the south fork of the Malheur River, a large party of Piutes, warriors, women and children, were camped on the border of Malheur Lake while the women gathered roots, herbs and seeds to dry for winter food. An epidemic came that was taking the lives of many, especially the children.

The Piute medicine men were unable to cope with it. There was much misery, women weeping, children dying and mothers grumbling against priests and beginning to doubt their potency.

It happened that a group of Bannocks from Idaho, or other points east, were visiting at the camp with the Piutes. The medicine men, who were becoming discredited and feared they would lose the respect and confidence of the Piutes, in their extremity to save their faces and reputations, accused the visiting Bannocks of having cast a spell over the sick persons, and so eloquently pleaded their cause that the Piute warriors attacked the Bannocks and all but exterminated the entire party.

However, one or more—a small remnant—of the Bannock party, escaped death and returned to Idaho.

Upon being told of the cruel massacre of their tribesmen and the reason for it, Bannock warriors assembled a large party and started for Malheur Lake with the intention of avenging the death of their fellows. When the invading party was yet several days off and in camp, Coyote slipped into camp, and overheard the boasts of the Bannocks and of their intention to kill the entire band of Piutes. The Coyote, being a friend of the Piutes, ran ahead of the approaching invaders and warned the Piutes, telling them of the overwhelming numbers and advising the Piutes to take refuge in some safe place, as they could not hope to withstand the invaders. The Coyote told the Piutes of Malheur Cave with its living water, where, even though they were less in numbers, they could hold out against the greater odds.

The Piutes heeded the advice of the Coyote, gathered up their supply of food and camp equipment and hurried to the cave. They barricaded the entrance with rocks and, although the warring Bannocks discovered the Piutes, the Piutes were able to keep them off. At first the Bannocks believed they could starve the Piutes and, not knowing of the water and food supplies, remained around the mouth of the cave for days, sending hundreds of obsidian-pointed arrows into the entrance and around the mouth of the cave.

After many days the invading party withdrew and the Coyote followed them on their eastern journey for a few days, finally returning to his Piute friends with the assurance that their enemy was well out of the country and it was safe for them to come out.

The Piutes removed only enough of the rocks to provide an exit, and that's how the entrance of Malheur Cave was found barricaded by the first white men and the reason for the presence of hundreds of arrowheads at its mouth and for some distance back into the cave.

That, also, is why the Piutes, in the long ago, revered the Coyote and would not kill him. He was considered the wisest, slyest, and most *cunning of the animals.*[4]

We hadn't seen another person since our early-morning encounter with the rancher and, because almost nothing for miles around stands higher than the sagebrush, we assumed that if there were other people around we would have seen them. We were alone on the bottom of a vanished sea, just the three of us and the sagebrush and the birds and animals. At the mouth of the cave, though, a big new Honda motorcycle with Nevada license plates glittered in the sunlight. A moment later we heard the growl of an engine from deep in the cave, and another motorcycle, this one a smaller version of the first and carrying two men, burst into the sunlight.

"You're gonna need lights," they told us. "It's huge. Bleachers. In there about a quarter of a mile. Seat four or five hundred people..." Still shaking their heads in amazement, they roared off across the desert.

They were right. It is huge. And it's dark. Our bicycle lights with their wheel-driven generators couldn't light the cave, so we took two propane lamps from the bus. Luke and Polly rode their bikes and I carried the lamps.

Malheur Cave is a lava tube, a fairly new lava tube, as geologists reckon time, formed only one or two million years ago. It is shaped, at its mouth, like a slightly squashed pipe with a diameter of about 25 feet. A modern petroglyph, a pair of calipers, symbol of the Masonic Lodge, is etched in white over the entrance.

Polly and Luke barrelled into the cave on their bikes. The sudden transition from sunlight to cavelight blinded me, but they rode confidently down toward the center of the earth, just as though they could see clearly where they were going. I brought up the rear, hustling along with a propane lantern in each hand and calling after them to be careful.

Just inside, the cave widens and the ceiling rises to a

height of about 20 feet. After a hundred feet or so, the cave branches. On the left, an area where the Indians might have kept horses. To the right, the cave continues, into the darkness.

About five hundred feet from the entrance, two sets of bleachers—four or five tiers high and about 80 feet long—face each other across an arena 25 or 30 feet wide. The bleachers are made of lumber—2x8s and 2x10s, mostly—set upon concrete blocks, and could probably, as the two bikers from Nevada had told us in their excitement, seat four or five hundred spectators. At the far end of the arena is a plywood stage, about 8 by sixteen feet, raised above the surface of the cave about two feet. Two stone podiums stand, like altars, centered, at opposite ends of the arena.

Clearly, we stumbled, deep in that cave, into the meeting place of some weird sect—modern Druids or Rajneeshees or some such. The little stone altars, perfect for sacrificing virgins or lambs, stood in mute testimony to the horrible ceremonies the cave had witnessed. We could see it all in our imaginations—flames from a ceremonial bonfire licking the air, shadows dancing on the ceiling, bleachers full of hooded devotees, sweating drummers pounding a delirious cadence, the Grand Dragon directing from the stage, sacrificial lambs, virgins, rabbits—something—chained, trembling, to the little altars, waiting, doomed, for the terrible ceremony to begin. The head wizard tests the tip of the sacred knife with his thumb, a bloodthirsty howl rises from the bleachers...

Just past the arena, the ceiling lowers, or, more precisely, the floor rises because of boulders and other chunks of lava littering the cave floor, so the cave seems smaller. Walking becomes more difficult, but a well worn trail leads through the boulders deeper into the cave. Polly and Luke left their bikes and we followed the trail. Two hundred feet or so beyond the stage, the floor of the cave dives into a subterranean lake or river. The water from this point on is wall to wall and extends far beyond the meager yellow glow or our propane lantern. A few feet offshore, a sign lay on the bottom of the lake. "Private property." Its letters wiggled up through little wavelets in the crystalline water. "No trespassing."

A few minutes later we'd picked our way back through the boulders and retrieved the bicycles. We stood outside the cave in the sunshine, alone again, wondering at what we'd seen down in that old lava tube. Later, we found that the bleachers were built by the Masonic Order of Burns, which owns the cave and has, since 1938, held its annual meeting there.

Back on the road again, and Polly is driving. I sit next to her—on the Coleman cooler, because the bus has no front passenger seat—but she is a good driver now and no longer needs my help, so I can watch the map and the scenery as we roll along. Later, Luke drives. He's not quite tall enough to reach the pedals, so he sits on my lap and mashes down on the accelerator with all his weight. Our children have sat on my lap to steer on country roads for years, but this is the first time with Luke that I haven't worked the pedals. Next year he'll be big enough to do it all and, with him, too, I'll graduate to the cooler in the middle of the bus.

From the cave we turn south, back to Highway 78, and then east, over the low north end of Steens Mountain. On the east side of the mountain we leave the highway and drive south on a wide, straight county road. We pass Folly Farm and Juniper Ranch and look for Alberson, a village which apparently exists only on the map. Soon Steens Mountain shows us its east face, a mile-high scarp jutting abruptly from the desert floor. The Steens—to our right—and Pueblo Mountains—now visible directly ahead, to the south—are basaltic blocks that rose along fault lines five to seven million years ago. Steens Mountain is the highest mountain in southeastern Oregon and the only one that held glaciers during the last ice age, which ended about 12,000 years ago.

To our left is Alvord Valley, a block that fell at the same time Steens Mountain and the Pueblo Mountains were rising. It's dry now, vast and flat and covered with sagebrush, but when the first men entered this part of Oregon, probably about 9-11,000 years ago, Alvord Valley was the bottom of a huge lake. Terraces or beaches, cut by waves as the lake receded are visible still along the edge of the valley, and early man found refuge here in caves eroded by the receding waves.

The road is straight and ours the only vehicle. Polly and Luke trade off driving. Down the road, hot water surfaces near the road and runs downhill to two little concrete pools. We stop and soak, contemplate solitude and quiet and the huge black clouds bumping around the east side of the mountain. A rickety sheetmetal and 2x4 structure riddled with bulletholes, some of them fired from inside, encloses one of the pools and a small dressing area. The kids wonder when cowboys get off work. They don't want to be in the pool when a mob of pistol-toting madmen shows up for a soak.

"STOP AIDS" is stenciled on the door to the enclosed pool. A circle with a diagonal line through it, like a European traffic sign, takes us a while to figure out. In the circle, a stick figure of a person bends over; another stands straight behind the first. Both face right. Polly figures it out first: "No sex."

"Hurry, Dad. Some cowdudes are comin'." Polly and Luke are dressed and waiting for me to pull on my clothes so we can get on down the road. I step out of the little dressing area and see two men coming down the path. Not cowdudes, just tourists.

We turned around and drove north a few miles and then pulled off into the sagebrush for the night. Dinner tonight: baked beans, Spam, canned peaches, chips. Breakfast tomorrow: fig bars, peanut butter and honey sandwiches, an orange.

The desert's green in April. There's a soft wind blowing

from the south tonight. Raining again, under leaden skies.

Wednesday:

I'm up alone this morning. Hot Lake steams in the east a mile or two away. We might have gone closer last night, but we were fooled by a padlock on a chain. We assumed that the chain went clear through the gate when it did not. A cowboy trick.

Steens Mountain looms in front of me. Behind me a barbed wire fence slices through the desert, north to south, for miles, straight as a line on paper. A few cows bawl behind the fence. They were clustered at the gate when we arrived, curious, I guess, but ran when Luke approached the gate. There was a fire here in the last year or so, judging from the charred condition of some of the sagebrush, but it's come back and is now damp and green over the black.

This is the bottom of an ancient lake and the Indian who lived here six or nine thousand years ago would not have sat where I am sitting, but may have passed over this spot in his canoe. He would have looked out over the water from the hillside over there where I can see the terraces left by the lap-lap of the waves as they receded. What would he have thought of us—a blue school bus parked on his lake bed, our little lawn chairs, Waylon and Willie and the Beach Boys serenading us from the tape deck, fire in a Coleman stove and the three mountain bikes that we explore the desert with? Surely the sun crept down the east face of those hills, just as it's doing now, warming him as it's warming me. He'd have thought we were a bad dream or some trick of Coyote's. He'd have been delighted, though, by this little herd of easy-to-catch meals bawling behind the fence.

I imagine him loping along the beach over there, carrying his atlatl and spear, looking for food to take back to his family. They're sheltered in a cave, maybe in those rocks, as mine is sheltered here in our old bus. He'd have felt good, I think,

45

because it's April now and warm, another winter behind him and he'd know that it'll be a long time before he'll feel cold again. He'll feel chilly, of course, on cool mornings, but the bone-chilling cold that comes to this country in December and January is behind him. Even the tempering effect of an inland sea probably didn't add much to the comfort of a man who lived in a cave and warmed himself with a tiny fire. He wore sandals, blankets, and skirts made from tules and sagebrush bark.

I hear geese this morning. To him that sound might have meant a meal.

Evening now:

We took our bikes through the gate and on down the road to Hot Lake. The Chinese mined, or scraped, borax here during the early part of this century. A couple of huge vats remain on the lakeshore. These were fired with sagebrush, and when all the sagebrush around had been burned, the operation closed down.

We swam and slithered around the lake in the mud and felt clean when we got out.

Polly drove into Fields, first time she'd ever driven in a town.

"You like to fish?" Elbows on the counter, we await World Famous Milkshakes in the Fields Restaurant. Polly and Luke, city-wary of the garrulous old stranger who sat a few seats away, instinctively shrink away from him, but, yes, they admit shyly, they like to fish. "I know where you can catch cutthroat trout. Native cutthroats."

They glance at each other, evidently deciding, simultaneously, that a man with that kind of news couldn't be all bad. "Where?" they ask.

Soon we were miles out in the country in the foothills of the Trout Creek Mountains, camped next to a small butte. A narrow creek, full of beaver dams made from willow branches, ran in a little cutbank ravine to our left. Just down the road in front of us was another of those cowboy miracles, a hot spring dammed up into a couple of pools, warm and hot.

We fished in the creek and lay around in the hot spring. Ralph, Polly and Luke's friend in Fields, told us we'd catch native cutthroat trout. Polly had one out of the water, "...and he was BIG!" Tears in her eyes. He fell off. I got one bite but had better luck and we ate mine for dinner.

On our bike ride this morning, Polly ran over a snake and we followed a lizard for awhile. Down by the hot spring we found a lizard who was not afraid of us. I touched his tail and he posed on a rock for pictures for us for a long time. We were going down to the hotspring for an after dinner soak, but some cowdudes have come and we'll wait for them to leave.

Thursday:

Willow Creek's just a gash in a great sagebrush-filled basin. Except for the leafy green tops of an occasional willow, you would not know it was there unless you fell into it.

We are camped on the west side of a nameless butte, so what morning sun there is has yet to reach us. I started a little a little sagebrush fire and a big red bull came to investigate. Red-winged blackbirds sing from the tops of the sagebrush. Polly and Luke have gone off after the fish that eluded them yesterday. Now another bull, this one a Brahma cross, ambles up out of the sagebrush. They stand together checking me out. Clouds scud across the sky and it looks like the rainy ones will go around us. Most of the trip's been like this.

Thinking again about the ancient hunter. This was probably a lake, too, in those days. I can see the terraces across the basin on the ancient beaches and this little butte behind me was a rocky islet. For him, life was simple. Find food. Eat. Shelter in a cave. I would not want to trade places. Sleeping in a cave all winter with only a sagebrush-bark blanket for warmth holds little appeal for me, but there is great appeal in a simpler life. I could, for instance, live like this, I think. We're all cavemen underneath. Some of us just have fewer layers to strip away. The strike is an eye-opener. There's more than one way to make a living, to live.

(It's all so clear and easy to see and rationalize when I'm over there. I remember thinking this one morning, after coffee, squatting over a little hole I'd dug in the sand near a juniper tree. Miles of sagebrush, juniper trees all over the place older than Christ, Pine Mountain just over there so clear I could reach out and touch it, the sun warming my bones while a desert wind whistled up my butt and I could lay out the whole rest of my life from there and see it just as clear as if it were on the wall in front of me on a chart. My job, now, and maybe for the rest of my life, is to write and make a living doing it. I've known it for a long time. But, next thing you know, the clearly rational me is checking the oil and climbing in the bus and heading west, back to work on Monday.)

Rain! Kids scamper back. Hail rattles on the bus and we run for the hot pool. With just our noses out of the water we are warm. Hailstones hit the surface of the little pool and then melt. STOP AIDS. There it is, stenciled on a rock above the pool. The storm marches off across the desert, shafts of sunlight play in the gray-green of the sagebrush. The wind dies and we are basking once again in sunshine.

(We came back to the Trout Creek Mountains the following March, Chris and the kids and I. Most days you could sit here all day in full view of a hundred or so square miles of sagebrush and never see another person. Suddenly this little hot spring became a convention center for southeastern Oregon.

Three little cars pulled up just down the road. These were cars that had never seen a rock, let alone an entire road made of dirt, the kind of little car that gets washed every Saturday morning and polished regularly every month. The people in them looked like that, too—like they'd taken a wrong turn on the way to a tennis tournament or a bridge match, and they'd never before been so far from the pavement. Five people from the first car, including a Dutch lady and her daughter, wandered by, peered over the rim of the pool at us like we were specimens in an aquarium. Five more people got out of the second car and wandered by as the first group had, peering over the rim of the pool at us. Then a white pickup pulled up. A couple of cowboys from the White Horse Ranch, working their way up the creek tearing out beaver dams, wondered what was bathing in the spring. They talked to the folks from the little cars, howdy'd us and headed on up the creek.

Our kids were splashing about and Chris and I were just sitting on a couple of rocks enjoying the scenery and the warm water and fifteen people were wandering about like they were looking for their first-ever tent site, peering occasionally at us in the pool like they'd like to get in but weren't sure the water was clean enough and, besides, the water was full of aliens.

They drifted away and I looked up and saw four more people walking toward the spring. This group appeared one at a time at the top of a little ridge near the spring and marched single file down the hill. As they got closer, I could see that each carried a rifle. Then I noticed that they were all dressed in green and brown camouflage fatigues and green and brown Australian bush hats. At first I thought they were hunters, but then I realized it was March and hunting season isn't until August at the earliest. I looked closer. Bandoleers loaded with ammunition criss-crossed on their chests, and each had a hog-leg pistol slung in a big, old-west style holster from a wide leather belt. An enormous beer belly slopped over every gunbelt buckle. They marched right up to the spring and I saw that their rifles were all semi-automatic, like M-14s, but smaller. This was a regular little guerrilla army. Che Guevara and the slobs.

The collegiate types suddenly lost interest in the hot spring. Their little cars were gone.

"Hope we're not driving you folks away," I heard as we headed for the bus. The army leaned its rifles against a big rock and unbuttoned its camouflage fatigue shirts, a relief, I'm sure, for the buttons that strained against those bellies.

"Oh, no," I smiled. "We were just leaving." Beneath the battle gear they wore pink long-johns.

About five miles up the road, far enough, I thought, that no one would follow us, we spent the rest of the afternoon fishing and writing and reading. After dinner that night, as we were climbing into bed, Chris saw headlights way down the road. The main road up there is hardly a road at all, and we were on a secondary road and I thought there's no way they'd choose that, but they did.

We saw them coming and turned off the lights. They came on by close enough to touch. "Hi, kids," one of them hollered, and then, "Hey. That's the kids we scared away earlier." They went on up the road and we waited for them to come on back and attack, but their lights disappeared over a ridge and we didn't see them again.

There was an intangible badness about that bunch. They looked crazy, sloppy, cruel. They didn't do anything, but they were scary. "Trust your instincts," we tell kids. "If something seems wrong or dangerous, it probably is." That's how I felt— instinctively that something was wrong, weird, dangerous.

We went back to the hot spring the next morning and sat out a hailstorm in the warm water. It was all peaceful and deserted again, just a million acres of sagebrush and fresh air and us. Someone left a 25-gallon barrel there for a garbage can. It was newly shot full of holes.)

We left the hot springs that afternoon. Back in Fields, Ralph is interested in the kids' fishing success. They are determined to return sometime and do better. We climb west from Fields, over the southern end of Steens Mountain and descend into Catlow Valley.

Friday:

How do they get these things so straight? We're parked beneath a powerline, three lines carried by a double set of poles with one crossbar, like two-legged Ts, they march out across the plain in one direction, off toward Steens Mountain in the other, and they are laid out so straight and plumb that each seems to fit inside the other, clear to where they disappear. I didn't notice the power line till after we'd stopped last night, but I could hear it when the wind picked up and made the wires moan.

Meadowlarks trill in the early morning calm. We're parked on the edge of a ravine that looks as though it should run with water at some time of the year, but, since this is the time and there is no water, perhaps it is an ancient riverbed, as this is an ancient lakebed.

We climbed to the top of Catlow Rim. This is special, I tell Luke and Polly, because for as far as they can see, hundreds of square miles, we are the only people visible. Man's works we can see—a few dirt roads, some small reservoirs, a powerline and some fences—but we are the only people. Just last month they visited San Francisco and Los Angeles and San Diego. They say they appreciate the difference.

A few minutes later Polly and Luke were rabbiting—jumping like rabbits, one foot out and flying ten feet down the slope—way ahead of me, when they stopped to examine something. When I caught up, Polly handed me a skull they'd found in the grass. It had been there a long time, from the look of it. It was long and narrow and worn-looking, bleached white by the sun and wind and rain and speckled brown where dirt caked on it. The cranial part was about the size of a tennis ball.

The front, snout, part was gone, chewed away by mice or eroded by time and weather. I told them I thought it was probably an antelope skull and they bounded away, on to the next event.

I stayed, though, curious about the creature whose skull I held in my hand. I looked for other bones, clues that would tell me more about it, about the manner, the drama, of its death, but I found none. There were no incisors or canine teeth, but the molars remaining in the skull were worn down from chewing, so the skull probably belonged to an old animal. Maybe, during the cold of winter its owner just lay down there on the hillside and died. Maybe a coyote or a mountain lion dragged him down as he ran across the hillside and the death of this creature meant survival for a predator or two. Maybe he was already dead when the coyotes found him and his bones were dragged up into the rimrocks to be shared.

The kids laughed as they loped through the grass where the slope leveled out near the road. The bus was just a little blue dot on a faraway road in the vast field of my vision, and Polly was to drive it alone for a few hundred yards up the road where they would pick me up.

This is a good place to die, I thought. High up here on the Catlow Rim, the creature whose skull I held looked his last at the incredible Catlow Valley. On this particular day rainstorms marched to and fro across the valley and the sky was awash with sweeping blues and grays and the arrogant slash of sunlight between the storms. The valley floor was a delicate gray-green, sagebrush newly washed as far as the eye could see. Meadowlarks and yellow-headed blackbirds lent their song to the wind, fine music, surely, for anyone's last dance in this world, and—breathe deep—my creature's last breath, as he lay his head on a soft cushion of grass and wildflowers, was from an ocean of clear, sage-scented air.

When I was young, too young to think about such things,

my father told me that when Death came to him he wanted to be fishing. I pictured him on McKay Creek some warm fall day, plunking a worm—he was a bait fisherman—into a hard-to-reach hole under the branches of a red sumac bush that grew from the bank when Death appeared beside him, knee-deep in the creek. My dad would look up, surprised at first, then, recognizing the inevitable, turn and be gone.

Dad didn't get his wish. Like most of us these days, he died in a hospital. I wasn't there when he died, but I imagine him lying in a hospital bed like others I've seen, stuck full of tubes in a room full of little beeping machines with video displays of his vital functions. He was surrounded by strangers at the end, a little circle of medical technicians and nurses, their surgical-masked faces hovering round him as they tried to get his heart started again. His last breath was not of the pine-scented eastern Oregon air that he loved. It came to him through an oxygen mask.

And Death? Well, Dad never knew what hit him, never felt any pain, they said—a thought that comforts me less than it does most people, I guess, because that was an experience my father would not have wanted to miss. He wasn't afraid of pain and he wasn't afraid of Death. He wanted to see Death coming, and probably took as little comfort as I in the thought of sliding away, feeling no pain, in a drug-induced coma.

Like my dad, I want to see Death when he comes for me. I'd like to be clambering around the rimrocks in the Blue Mountains a few miles from Ukiah, though I guess this spot, high up on Catlow Rim, would do as well. When Death comes, I'll turn and recognize him, look him square in the eye and take his measure before he has his way with me. If I'm lucky, there won't be anyone else around, no one to call for a helicopter so I can be rushed to an emergency room and die as my dad did, full of tubes and surrounded by strangers.

Ideally, no one will find my body. Coyotes and vultures

and a host of lesser creatures will use what they can, scatter my bones around, and I'll be up there in the rimrocks forever—a thought far more comforting than that my body might be found immediately, dragged off to a mortuary, pumped full of chemicals and planted for eternity in a plush and expensive cloth-covered metal box.

Later, after they quit looking for me, someone will put up a marker down by the road. The marker—I'd call it a tombstone, but there's no tomb in this fantasy—will say that Mike Helm met Death up there, somewhere. His body was never found, his bones were probably scattered by coyotes, and he now lies on the part of the earth that he loved above all the rest.

I imagine some grandchild of mine bringing his children to the marker down along the road near Ukiah. "That was your great-grandfather," he'll say. "Mike Helm. He met Death up there somewhere. He was stone cold sober, and he looked Death square in the eye and took his measure..."

The Blue Goose churned down the road toward me, Polly, triumphant, at the wheel, driving for the first time without me beside her. She pulled the bus up smartly beside where I stood at the side of the road and when the door opened Luke cheered, as pleased with his sister as she was with herself.

After a stop in Frenchglen for a a a can of pop and a phone call home, we drive toward the P Ranch Headquarters on the Malheur National Wildlife Refuge. The Refuge, one of the largest in the United States, is shaped like a large T, with Frenchglen at the bottom of the stem. Its 184,000 acres stretch more than 40 miles north to Malheur Lake and include the largest freshwater marsh in the United States. Countless birds and animals make their homes here, either on a seasonal or year-round basis, making the Refuge a major attraction for bird watchers and other lovers of wildlife.

Luke and Polly have been to the Refuge many times. They are keen-eyed wildlife observers. When we were here in December, the land was coated with a thin layer of snow. We encountered herds of mule deer, great flocks of Canada geese and, as we sat on the rimrocks above a pond on the way to Krumbo Reservoir one morning, five swans sailed in below us. Later, we walked across the pond on the ice, and Luke fell through. We watched, fascinated, one afternoon as a coyote prowled the ice far out on Malheur Lake within sight of the refuge headquarters. Luke howled into the night and was delighted when coyotes answered from the hills all around. Another afternoon we watched a pair of coyotes mousing in a meadow on the southern part of the refuge. But we don't hear coyotes this trip and none are visible.

The Malheur National Wildlife Refuge is a major nesting area for the greater sandhill crane, which is classified as a "sensitive" species, that is, a species that will become threatened or endangered if the trend toward a diminished population is not reversed. The number of greater sandhill cranes nesting on the refuge declined from 236 pairs in 1971 to 181 in 1986. Studies show that ravens and raccoons are responsible for predation of the eggs, and that coyotes eat many of the chicks before they're old enough to fly. In some years, according to a refuge press release, as few as 2 chicks from nearly 200 nesting pairs have survived to leave the refuge in the fall.

In September, 1985, the folks who manage the Refuge announced a controversial program to control ravens, raccoons, and coyotes for three years, in the hope of reversing the decline in the number of greater sandhill cranes on the refuge. Control, of course, means kill.

In the three years of that program's existence, 852 coyotes have been controlled (That is, 580 coyotes were shotgunned from low-flying aircraft, 138 killed using traps and snares, 92 killed by calling and shooting, and 49 by denning. Denning means finding the coyote den in the spring and killing the pups before they leave. Pups are dug out, smoked out--a bellows-operated bee smoker with a length of garden hose attached is good for smoking coyote pups out of their dens—or hooked out with a wire cable by twisting the frayed cable end into their fur. If the pups simply cannot be frightened, smoked or dragged out to be clubbed to death, they can easily be poisoned by throwing a handful of calcium cyanide into the den and stopping up the hole. In this particular program, the pups were suffocated when a gas cartridge was placed in the den, the entrance covered with dirt. The cartridge consumed the oxygen in the den. One must be careful that the mother doesn't escape.) as have approximately 286 ravens (Dead ravens are hard to find, and therefore, except for the 16 ravens known to have been shot by government hunters during the three years of this program, this number is an estimate based on an expected ratio of one dead raven for every dozen poisoned eggs left for them to eat.) and 39 raccoons (Ten hunted with dogs, ten shot, 19 caught in snares, live traps, and leghold traps.).

In the fall of 1988, at the conclusion of the predator control program, all the sandhill cranes left the reservation before they could be counted. Casual observations, according to the Executive Summary report, indicated that there was high chick mortality late in the season, from unknown causes but probably related to dry conditions, that offset any gains made early in the year. Tallies from previous years show the sandhill crane population continuing to decline. The predator control program, though, was judged successful by Refuge personnel and will be continued for another five years.

(I returned in 1989 and 1990. Nights are quieter now on the Malheur National Wildlife Refuge.)

Clouds to the east, clear sky to the west, a good omen, since we will be going west today, home, to the city, to the strike. No meadowlarks tomorrow. What a wonderful, mind-clearing experience is this strike.

Monday, Monday. Post-strike Monday:
   That country's sure got a hold on me. One of these days
the hook'll be set a little too deep and I won't make it back. At
each westward turn on our return trip every atom in my body
was screaming "East. Go east!" The clearly rational me, though,
headed west and brought the rest of me along. The clearly
rational me will go to work this morning, too. But the rest of me
is out there in the sagebrush prowling coyote dens and hot
springs and climbing to the top of those rimrock bluffs and
fantasizing and writing about Oregon. I've been coming back
to this overcrowded Willamette valley "for just a little longer"
since 1960. I never figured 28 years'd go by and I'd still be
fighting this battle with myself.

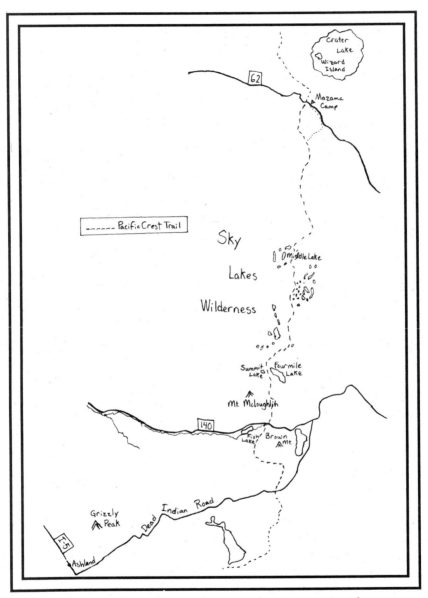

Pacific Crest National Scenic Trail
Dead Indian Road to Crater Lake

The Sky LakesWilderness

or

How the Mosquitoes Taught Me to Hike

"An old rule of thumb says you can carry a third of your body weight. An indeed, if you have to, you can..."
  John Hart
  Walking Softly in the Wilderness

Spring, 1987. Hot, summerlike weather. My heart was in the wilderness, but my body was in the classroom with Henry David Thoreau and my sophomore global literature classes.

"Advance confidently," Thoreau told us, "in the direction of your dreams." I dreamed of advancing, south to north, along the Pacific Crest Trail from the California border to the Columbia River. I wasn't an experienced hiker and I hadn't trained for this hike, but I knew all I had to do to complete it was to attack it in segments and keep moving. My first stretch of the Pacific Crest Trail (PCT) ran from where the PCT crossed Dead Indian Road, 28 miles east of Ashland, to Crater Lake.

Day 1 — June 23, 1987 — 5300 feet:

I said goodbye to Chris and the kids at the front gate at 6:30 this morning. They stood in a little group and looked sad and I felt bad leaving them. I wonder what they think of this trip.

I arrived at the Greyhound station in Ashland at 3:20. While I was trying to figure out how to get to the trailhead on Dead Indian Road I went to the Chamber of Commerce and asked if any local buslines went that way. They didn't. The lady was trying to find Dead Indian Road on a map when a young man, a wild-looking redhead, said, "I can show you. You looking for the Pacific Crest Trail?"

"Yup."

"Not far. You afraid of motorcycles?"

"Nope."

"I'll take you there."

"My pack weighs 90 pounds."

"That's okay."

So he did. He took me the last 28 miles on the back of a motorcycle. When he accelerated, the pack tried to pry me off the back of his bike. The wind was a constant pull, the pack taking it like a sail.

"Which of these hills is Grizzly Butte?"

"I don't know."

But there it was, just north or Dead Indian Road, Grizzly Peak on the map. I'd heard of Grizzly Butte:

During the second Rogue River War, in 1855-56, my brother Henry, with two neighbors, was out in the hills looking for hostile Indians. He saw several grizzly bears on the hillside eating service berries. Henry was a good shot. He had a hard-shooting muzzle-loading gun. He took careful aim and shot at one of the largest of the bears. It fell in its tracks. He loaded his gun and shot another bear, which made off in the direction taken by the other bears.

Henry, carelessly, did not reload his gun, but went up to examine the dead bear, which was a huge one. Just as he got to it the bear came to and made for Henry. Henry started to run. The bear struck at him, tearing Henry's coat nearly off. Henry ran for a tree, which proved too large for him to climb. He ran toward a smaller tree, but the bear overtook him and with one blow knocked him down and tore his shoulder blade loose. The bear with one or two strokes of his claws tore Henry's clothes off.

Henry had heard an Indian say that if a grizzly attacked you if you 'memaloosed' the bear would leave you alone, so Henry played dead. The bear had never heard that bears do not molest dead men, for he bit my brother in the loins and back so that Henry screamed from the pain. Then the bear clawed his head and turned him over to bite his neck. My brother rammed his fist into the bear's mouth. The bear crushed the bones in his hand and wrist. Then the bear bit him through the shoulder and stripped the flesh from one leg from the thigh to the knee.

Two young men with my brother heard him scream when the bear bit him in the loins and hurried back. They shot and killed the grizzly.

My brother was still conscious, and as they rolled the bear off him he said, "I'll never see Mother or Father or old Kentucky again." Then he fainted. They thought he was dead, so they tied him across his horse to bring him in for a Christian burial. The motion of the horse brought him to.

They took him to the home of 'Daddy' Wells, a nearby settler. There was no doctor nearer than Jacksonville, so one of the boys rode at full speed to get the doctor, while Daddy Wells washed my brother's wounds and with a sack needle and twine sewed the flesh that was hanging loose back into place. When the doctor came he had to rip out all the stitches so as to wash the torn flesh better.

Henry's neck was terribly lacerated. They thought he could not live, but he kept alive day after day and at last they decided to send him to San Francisco to secure the services of a surgeon to fix his shoulder, which was so badly shattered when the bear crunched it that the local doctor could not fix it. Even the San Francisco surgeon could not restore its strength and usefulness...

They still call the mountain where the bear and my brother had their fight Grizzly Butte. Come out on the porch and I will point out Grizzly Butte to you.[1]

In the old days, grizzlies walked and talked like men and carried huge sticks, but they angered Old Man Above, who created the Shasta world, and life for the grizzlies hasn't been the same since. It happened like this:

The wind blew so hard that it blew the smoke down the smoke hole in Old Man Above's teepee, which we call Mt. Shasta. Old Man Above told his daughter to climb up to the smoke hole and tell the wind to quiet down. He cautioned her to signal the wind by waving her arm from the smoke hole before she spoke to the wind. The little girl was excited to see the world, though, and she forgot the warning and put her head through the smoke hole first.

The wind grabbed her by the hair, pulled her out of the smoke hole, blew her down the mountain and left her, half-frozen, close to the teepee of the grizzlies. Soon the grizzlies returned home and found the little girl. They carried her into their teepee where they warmed her by the fire and fed her and cared for her until she was well again.

The girl did not return to Old Man Above's teepee, but stayed with the grizzlies. She grew up, fell in love with one of the young grizzlies, and married him. The grizzly family built a fine teepee for the new couple. We call that teepee Little Shasta.

Soon children were born to the couple. The children were not grizzlies, though, but men.

The mother grizzly one day sent one of her sons to Old Man Above to tell him that his daughter was alive. When Old Man Above heard this news, he climbed out of the smoke hole and ran down the mountainside so fast that, wherever he set his foot, the snow melted and gushed down the mountainside.

The grizzlies stood to greet Old Man Above, and were surprised to see that he was enraged by the sight of the daughter and her children, this new race, man. To punish the grizzlies for their part in the creation of man he told them that they could never speak again and that from this time forward, they would walk on four legs and look downward as they walked. He put out the fire in the teepee, and drove the new race of man out into the world where men have lived ever since. Then he grabbed his daughter by the hand and led her back to his teepee.[2]

But that was long ago. Grizzlies have been extinct in Oregon since 1931, and I mourn their passing.

I'm sitting on a stump five feet in diameter just uphill from the Pacific Crest Trail about four miles north of Dead Indian Road. I started hiking about 5 p.m., quit about 6:45.

This is harder than I thought it would be. I spend much time going over an inventory in my mind of stuff I can do without. My feet hurt already. The first post office I come to, I'll send a package back home.

The sun is setting and I am about to eat my reconstituted chili—which did not, near as I can tell, reconstitute except to the form of a soup with little rubber balls of meat.

Too tired to put up a tent tonight, so I'm putting my trust in Cutter's mosquitoe repellent, which has so far served me well. No clouds anywhere as the sun sets. I don't think rain will be a problem.

I camp tonight in a clearcut, an abomination, man-made, in the middle of a second-growth forest. Stumps like the one on which I sit dot the landscape like tombstones in a high mountain graveyard. My bed is a flat spot made by a Caterpillar tractor some muddy day long ago.

And now the sun sets, with Brown Mountain dead ahead to be passed tomorrow.

Day 2 —June 24, 1987—6:30 a.m.:

I went to bed with the sun last night, but the sun rose before me this morning. A little hummingbird, sounding like a distant chain saw, was working the purple flowers near my ear when I awoke. Now I'm sitting on the stump watching the sun creep into the forest across the clearcut.

I checked for aches left from my four-mile warmup and found none too serious, though there are a few. The blister on the bottom of my left foot is the most serious potentially, so I'll be careful with it today. The belt from my pack bruised me around the points of my pelvis and I'll have to tough that one out. I don't know if I can do 20 miles today, but I'll have a go.

5:15 p.m.

I never dreamed it would be so tough. I started out feeling strong enough this morning, but within a mile my whole body was pleading with me to quit. Each step came jarring down, driving my leg like a fencepost into the ground. The belly strap on the pack knifed into my waist. On the uphill my leg muscles screamed with pain and on the downhill I seemed to lose all grace and I staggered and each slipshod step tore at the blisters on the bottom of my left foot. I am slow to learn, but learn I have: 90 pounds is too much.

It is eleven miles from Dead Indian Road to where I am now and every foot of that way I inventoried and rationalized getting rid of some of my burden. A couple of times, after resting, I could just barely get my pack on.

When I arrived here about 1:30 I did some serious repacking, sorting out a pile of extra stuff that nearly filled the pack by itself. I stashed the rest of my gear behind a tree, uphill from the Pacific Crest Trail, and walked about a mile and a half to Fish Lake Resort, where a very nice lady found a box for me to pack it in. She will send it home for me via UPS next time someone goes to Medford. The box weighed 28 pounds. Then I loaded up on water—one quart in my belly and three quarts in canteens—and came back up here. It was nearly four by then, so I decided to stay the night right, just above the trail and within hearing of the Highway 140. I lay down and fell asleep in spite of the incessant whine of the mosquitoes.

The mosquitoes we know are the descendants of Wawa, a mosquito god who terrorized people in the time of the ancients. Wawa was larger than any man and his needle was three or four feet long and very sharp and terrible. He lived in mountain passes, and when anyone wanted to pass through his territory, Wawa, thrust his enormous needle like a sword into the body of the traveler and sucked out all his blood.

Coyote was traveling one day up in Washington when he heard of this terrifying creature. Wawa had made the people afraid to travel, so Coyote knew he must do something. "I will vanquish Wawa," he told the people, and he set out to do so.

Coyote had to travel quite a distance to find Wawa—Perhaps he met him right here, in the Sky Lakes Wilderness—and as he traveled he tried to think of a plan to defeat the monster. Though he thought and thought, he failed to come up with a good plan, so he decided to consult his sisters. He took the sisters out of his belly and asked them how to defeat Wawa. "Why should we tell you?" they asked. "You'll just claim that our idea was yours. We're not going to tell you."

"If you don't tell me, I'll call down the hail upon you," Coyote promised, glancing at the sky.

The sisters greatly feared being cold, and the threat to bring the hail always terrified them. "Wait. Don't bring the hail," they pleaded. "We'll tell you." Then they whispered a plan into Coyote's ear.

"Yes," he said, "that is just what I was going to do. That is my plan."

So Coyote put the sisters back into his belly where they would be warm. Then he gathered five kinds of wood to use as fire-rods, hid them inside his coat, and continued his search for Wawa.

Presently, he came to a mountain pass, where Wawa had his house. "Hold it! You can't pass through here," Wawa challenged him when he saw Coyote coming through the pass. "This is my pass. I allow no one to cross through here." Wawa charged menacingly toward Coyote, aiming his terrible proboscis toward Coyote's belly.

In a matter-of-fact way, Coyote held up his hand and said, "Wait, old friend. I've not come to harm you. I noticed that you had no fire and, because it is a cold day, I have brought wood. Let me build a fire in your house so that you can warm yourself."

The mosquito-god stopped and scratched his head. No one had ever treated him with kindness before, and he wasn't sure how to respond. He was very suspicious, but it was a cold day, and he thought how nice it would be to warm himself before a fire, so he said to Coyote, "Very well. You may pass into my house and build a small warming fire."

Coyote took out the first of his five fire rods and began to spin it, but no fire came. He spun the second fire-rod; still no fire. With the *third and the fourth he had the same result, but when he spun the fifth, fire blazed almost immediately. Coyote heaped it high with fuel and soon a huge fire raged in the mosquito-god's house. Wawa's house had no chimney and filled quickly with dense smoke. Wawa could not breathe, so he lay on the floor, hoping to get a breath of air from beneath the layer of smoke.*

Coyote, quick to press his advantage, grabbed a huge stone knife and leapt on top of the old mosquito-god. "You'll not kill people any more," he said as he raised the knife high over his head. "Your power is gone. From now on you may irritate and whine and take a little blood, but you will no longer be powerful." With terrible force he brought the stone knife down, splitting the monster's head open. From inside the head, dozens of little mosquitoes such as have existed ever since swarmed forth.

Since that time mosquitoes have been small and have not been able to stand smoke. With this lesson, Coyote taught the people to use smoke to protect themselves from mosquitoes.[3]

I don't think there's any part of me that doesn't hurt right now, from my aching head to the stinging blisters on the bottom of my left foot. I expected the first days to be tough, and I was right. I also expected to get stronger as I went along, and I'll wait for the verdict on that one. Losing 28 pounds from my pack, plus the pound or two that I've eaten should make the next few days easier.

The trail today crossed basalt flows from Brown Mountain. It was dramatic in some places and very well maintained, with newly-laid crushed rock along stretches of it, just a walk in the park if it weren't for this pack. I saw a couple of deer and a large Hungarian partridge.

On the trail down to the resort, water gushes down a basalt flow to a flat where beavers have dammed the stream and then it flows out and disappears into the basalt flow again.

Total miles so far: Pacific Crest Trail   11
                        Trail to Lake   <u>3</u>

Total   14

Dinner tonight: one cup of Minute Rice, one Campbell's veg, noodle and meatball Cupasoup, 2 boullion cubes, all mixed together. A good gruel.

Feelin' better now. Cutter's keeps the muzzies about four inches from my face where they swarm now, but they don't seem much interested in my legs.

In their book, The Pacific Crest Trail, Jeffrey P. Schaffer and Andy Selters say you could walk the whole Pacific Crest Trail carrying only a quart of water. Not so, at least for me, on a hot day. I drank a quart at the resort and two quarts since. Maybe water will be more easily available in the Sky Lakes Wilderness .

7 p.m.   Elevation 4940

The sun slants through the trees now. Last night it wasn't dark till after ten. The frog in the moon looked lonely last night.

I had stashed my gear above the trail in a low forest with a dry crunchy floor. When I returned from the resort I was too tired to move so I just left everything there and rolled out my sleeping bag. A couple of times I thought about investigating a little grassy meadow just below the trail, but ended up lying back down each time.

I recovered enough to have a look and then moved my gear down to the meadow, a rarity in this area, adjacent to one of Brown Mountain's huge basalt flows. The flows, enormous boulders placed in rows by the hand of God, stretch for miles. From here I can see the north side of Brown Mountain, just a huge pile of basalt, really, forested in patches all the way to the top.

The meadow is surrounded by a diverse array of trees and bushes—ponderosa pine, Douglas fir, white fir, I think, some alder and a bush that looks like madrone. The pines grow among the basalt boulders.

Day 3 —June 25, 1987—7:30 a.m.:
Didn't wake till seven. Having coffee now on this fabulous rockpile, warming my bones in the sun. I know I should get going earlier, but figure I'll get a better regimen going later in the hike when I'm not so sore and not so much in need of rest.

High thin clouds this morning. Hope they don't portend a change in the weather. Trucks and cars whizzing by on the highway which I haven't seen yet but know well by sound. But for that sound the nearest human might be miles away.

9:30 a.m. — Sky Lakes Wilderness
Stopped for breakfast—granola, sulphured apricots and some nut and raisin mix. Also drinking water purified with tablets. Tastes better than I thought it would.

The trail today goes up and up, ever upward, winding through an old growth fir forest that juts from the massive basalt flow I am traversing.

What a joy to lose 30 pounds. Today I walk instead of stagger. The waist belt on my backpack hugs my middle instead of knifing into it and my body sweats and tells me, "This is hard work," instead of screaming at me to stop. The blisters on the bottom of my foot still hurt, but not nearly with yesterday's intensity.

Somewhere on the trail ahead of me is a person on a horse, a smoker, with a typical smoker's lack of regard for where he tosses cigarette butts. The trail today is more a wilderness path than the carefully tended trail of yesterday, and it is what Schaffer and Selters call "essentially viewless", though I am beginning to think they sometimes do not see the forest for the trees. This is a lovely, elemental wilderness.

10:48 a.m.
Drenched with sweat. I love that feeling. Little rivulets dripping off my nose, running down my back. Still climbing. Can't believe I haven't passed the four mile mark yet.

Now I know why the author of Pacific Crest Trail only had a few 20 mile days, even after months on the Pacific Crest Trail. Twenty-plus miles might be possible after good conditioning and across flat terrain, but it's mighty difficult with hilly terrain and a pack even with the weight around 60 pounds.

I am sitting on a log beside the ascending trail in a parklike old growth forest. From here the trail climbs—and climbs and climbs, I think. Lots of downed trees are scattered among the massive standing trees, but the only evidence of a chainsaw is near the trail. Must have been a natural catastrophe years ago that broke them all off and left those snaggy stumps pointing skyward.

No wind. Only sunshine, though high clouds persist. Birds and insects are the only sounds.

Many deer tracks on the trail and much coyote and mountain lion scat, but the only wildlife I've seen since yesterday is a small flight of geese and one great blue heron that flew over my campsite this morning.

2:00 p.m.

Finally found a lake in the Sky Lakes Wilderness, so here I sit in the sun, clothed in my underpants because the horseflies were biting my butt. This is Summit Lake, eight miles from the highway, 47.5 miles to Crater Lake. This lake is a little north of the trail and was a disappointment when I first looked at it. A pond, really, not more than three feet deep anywhere, with a couple of dozen trees fallen into and around it. But the water felt good. I left my clothes on the bank and waded out and had my first good rinse-off since I showered Tuesday morning.

After eight miles yesterday there wasn't one single part of me that did not hurt. Today is better. The hurt is confined to blistered feet and my middle where the waist strap has bruised it. Nevertheless, progress is not what I'd hoped it would be. I've gone eight miles today. I'll do a few more after this midday rest period.

Danger! Cutter's Mosquito Repellent about half gone.

5:05 p.m.

I stopped here, about two miles from Summit Lake, for a rest. Sore feet and no mosquitoes, so I decided to stay the night. Thin overcast is thickening, as is my fear of rain. Mount McLoughlin, which I cannot find on my thin strip of a map, is visible from here, its north face spectacular with snow fields.

Mount McLoughlin was named for Dr. John McLoughlin, chief factor of the Hudson's Bay Company at Fort Vancouver from 1824 to 1846. It was called Mt. McLoughlin on a map issued in 1838, but on later maps was renamed Mt. Pit, for the Pit or Pitt River which was so named because of the pits Indians of this region dug to trap game. The Oregon Legislature restored the name Mt. McLoughlin in 1905.

For dinner: Minute Rice and Cupasoup again with a couple of boullion cubes added for flavor and whatever nutrition.

Let's see. All I have to do is walk 45 miles to Crater Lake carrying a 60 pound pack, on feet so sore I can barely walk the length of my sleeping bag.

Total Pacific Crest Trail miles so far—21.

Ten miles today. There won't be any 20 mile days for me. I could do it without the pack, I think, because it's not the walking that's killing me, it's carrying that damn pack.

Dumb things:

1. Bringing too much stuff — four shirts, for instance.

2. Wearing workboots. Next time I buy workboots, I'll wear them to work.

3. Bringing the Coleman anvilweight stove instead of our little Gaz stove.

4. Bringing our heavy 3-man tent instead of the lightweight 2-man tent.

Day 4—June 26, 1987—6 a.m.:

It was not yet dark, but I was in my sleeping bag reading when I heard him coming down the hill from the other side of the Pacific Crest Trail. He was crashing along, knocking over rocks and breaking dry branches, making as much noise as a whole herd of deer. I lay still and waited, hoping I'd soon have a herd of deer or elk right in my camp.

From my vantage point on the ground I could see beneath the lowest branches of a stand of little trees about ten feet on the other side of the trail. My first view of him was only his back half, from the side—of his amazing long, thick tail dropping to nearly touch the ground and then curling up at the end. He ambled on, and I had to move to see the rest of him on the other side of a small tree. As I moved, he turned toward me, apparently intending to cross this little clearing on a path that went right across my sleeping bag. He saw me then and stopped and dropped low into a crouch and froze. For the longest time we sat and looked at each other across that little space.

I don't know what he was thinking, but I was trying hard to remember every detail about him—his great oval face and green eyes and long tawny body. He was big. His paws were enormous, much larger than my fists, and his tail nearly as thick as my forearm. He looked fat, sleek, and healthy, well fed, probably on those deer whose tracks constantly betray their presence on the Pacific Crest Trail. I felt profoundly grateful to be there watching him watch me.

He looked a great deal, I think, like an African lioness crouched there, and it occurred to me after we'd watched each other for a while that he might be considering me for a late evening snack, so I reached over and unholstered my pistol, wondering, while I did, if it was really loaded.

Still he crouched and watched. I whistled and moved my arms. He watched, not moving. Finally I spoke to him. "Hi, there." That did it. He turned and crashed off through the brush, uphill from Pacific Crest Trail. A few minutes later I heard him snarling and spitting a hundred yards or so above from my camp. He moved across the hillside from my left to right, and then I heard him later on the same level as me as though he'd crossed the trail farther up and detoured around me, still intending to get down the hill to his destination.

Coyote was a great admirer of Mountain Lion. One day, when Coyote was out hunting, he came upon a small herd of deer browsing some low bushes in a meadow. He watched them for a long time, wishing he could think of a way to catch one, but knowing that it would be impossible for him, for they would easily outrun him.

Suddenly, a big rock rolled downhill toward them. The deer were frightened and ran a short distance, stopping when they realized it was only a rock. Another rock rolled down and they watched it but did not run away. Another, and then another rock rolled into the meadow. Coyote looked to the top of a hill and saw that Mountain Lion was rolling the rocks. The deer knew now that these were only rocks harmlessly rolling into the meadow, so they continued to browse, paying no attention.

Mountain Lion then curled himself into a ball and rolled downhill into the meadow, stopping right next to the biggest deer in the herd. Before the deer could see that this wasn't just another rock, Mountain Lion leapt onto his back and killed him. Mountain Lion then dragged the deer off into the brush to eat him.

The next day Coyote decided to borrow Mountain Lion's trick. He found a small herd of deer and rolled rocks downhill toward them until they were so accustomed to rolling rocks that they no longer ran away. Then he curled himself into a ball and rolled downhill and across the meadow, stopping next to the plumpest deer in the herd. When he tried to stand up and catch the deer, he was so dizzy that he fell on his face and the deer ran away.

8:15 a.m.

Stopped for breakfast. On the trail this morning at 7:15. Last night was the worst yet for sleep. As I get stronger, it's harder to fall asleep.

Last night I was thinking that Shaffers and Selter had overstated the mosquito problem, that all I had to do was sleep away from the lakes to avoid the mosquitoes. I was wrong. Though I never saw a musquito there in the late afternoon, and, consequently, decided to stay the night without putting my tent up, when darkness crept in so did the mosquitoes. Cutter's failed to dissuade them and they stayed all night, biting and whining and keeping me awake.

Ripping along now, almost to Red Lake Trail. I am wearing my old tennis shoes, boots in my backpack. The old blisters hurt a little, but it doesn't feel like walking on hot coals like yesterday and I'm not all the time wearing new blisters as the boots were doing.

Soon after I left camp this morning I came across a couple of tree frogs, one bright green to match the foliage where I saw him and another brown, like the dirt, who jumped over the trail, pissing a bright golden arc that caught the morning sun. I also ran into a new breed of mosquito that attacked me one by one as I moved, unlike other mosquitoes so far. They seemed also to like Cutter's.

9:45 a.m. — Island Lake

Surely this place is one of the rewards of this trek. I'm sitting on a rock on the grassy shore of this lake, for some reason a mosquito-free zone. The lake is about 300 yards across and about 100 yards from where I sit on the east shore is the little island from whence it apparently gets its name. Last night I heard avalanches rumbling down Mt. McLoughlin. This morning I see dark brown streaks across the mountain's snowy face.

Near me, bright blue dragon flies mate with their gray,

drab-looking partners—their enjoyment of this act of creation apparent by the frenzied excess of energy with which they go about it in the early summer sunlight.

A sparrow with a black head and a mouth full of feathers flutters in the tree near me and a fish whacks the water a few feet offshore. A chipmunk, curious, watches me for awhile and then moves closer and closer, moving in quick little spurts—then, too close, dives off the log and disappears. Down the shore a great blue heron lifts off and flies across the lake.

Years ago a horrible witch who ate Indian children dwelt in the woods near here. She had long, sharp claws on her skinny hands and pointed teeth and cruel eyes that burned like fire in the night. Indian mothers carefully guarded their children, but the monster had a way of enticing them to her. Once they were away from their mothers, she devoured them like a coyote might devour a lamb.

For many years this witch terrorized the Indians and they could do nothing to stop her. One day she was about to eat a small child as the child's mother watched. The mother cried so hard and loud that Sahalee Tyee, the great spirit, heard and decided to intervene. Quickly, he transformed the child into a beautiful chipmunk that sprang out of the witch's grasp and ran away.

As the chipmunk raced from the witch, she grabbed at it with one thin hand. Her claws scraped down the chipmunks back, but he managed to escape. The black stripes down the chipmunk's back are the marks made by the cruel claws of the wicked witch.[4]

This place is so quiet—well, not quiet, but devoid of human noises that seem so intrusive here. Every noise I make—uncorking my canteens, dropping the lid of the water purification tablet bottle against a rock, even splashing as I enter the water and slap water on myself—seems to blare and screech against the backdrop of natural noise. Then a plane roars over, shattering the quiet everywhere and the noise of my intrusion is put back into perspective.

So, bathed and watered—a quart in my belly and three on my back—I'm on the road again.

Day 5—June 26, 1987— Sitting in my tent at Middle Lake: Mileage yesterday, 19.

Yesterday was the toughest yet. From Island Lake the trail wound up and up to run along the backbone of the Sky Lakes Wilderness. The wilderness is two lake basins separated by a north-south running range of mountains bout 7000-7500 feet in elevation. The trail climbs almost to the peaks and then runs northward along the saddles that connect them and across open talus slopes which drop steeply hundreds of feet on one side. The snow was not melted from the north-facing slopes and where it buried the trail and I crossed the snowfields I often had visions of the pack and I making a quick and slippery descent. The views were magnificent, even on a hazy, cloudy day.

For a while, at the top, there were no mosquitoes. Perhaps they can't fly at that altitude. But every time the trail descended through the forest they were there to greet me. A multitude of lakes, bogs, and little snowmelt streams ensures a multitude of mosquitoes. Most of the time, if I kept moving, they would not bite. If I stopped to rest in the shade, though, their cursed whining was in my ear in a second. I could rest (and bake) in the sun and then have only the flies, gnats, ants, and assorted other flying scourges to contend with for awhile. Then, slowly, one by one, the mosquitoes would venture into the sunlight to torment me. Insects keep me moving along the Pacific Crest Trail.

Along about suppertime, as I was hurrying to find water and a place to camp, I ran into another new breed of mosquito, one that attacked in huge clouds and didn't care if I was moving or stopped. I was still wearing shorts and descending into the lake basin on this side (west side) of the mountains. They were all over me, biting and whining and as fast as I wiped them off they were back on, drilling into my skin right through the carnage of their squashed and smeared brothers. I walked faster and faster and soon was nearly running down the trail. The faster I went, the faster they went, though, and they seemed determined to suck me dry. I finally realized that I couldn't outrun them, so I stopped, dropped my pack, and dug into it. I put on a long-sleeved, hooded sweatshirt and Levis, grabbed the Cutter's and smeared it over all exposed skin. They kept experimenting, but could not bite through the Levis if I kept moving. Cutter's kept them away from my face and hands.

When I arrived here I put up the tent and cooked up some rice and soup but was too tired to eat. I can't recall ever being too tired to eat before.

The tent earned its ride last night. I stretched out naked on my sleeping bag inside it and watched the mosquitoes cluster at the netting in little gangs, trying to find a way in. They stayed on duty all night, but never got in. I slept soundly and when I awoke they were still there—outside.

My old Nike shoes are far better on my feet than the boots, which have now become a five pound burden. I fully intended to burn them last night but was too tired. I don't want to carry them any more, but don't know what to do with them. I know I shouldn't, but maybe I'll just leave them hanging in a tree. (I did.)

Today, an easier day. I think I'll try to make it to Solace Cow Camp. Then Stuart Falls Camp the next day and then Crater Lake and home. For sure, today I'll leave this mosquito-infested lake basin behind.

9:50 a.m.

Mosquitoes seem to be taking a break, so I will, too. I'll even risk taking off my sweatshirt.

Today's hike started with a climb back to the Pacific Crest Trail and then a gentle descent. How I resent those downhill stretches. I practically sweat blood for every foot of elevation gain, only to give it all away after topping the next rise.

Breakfast. Granola and dried apricots again. I'm amazed at how many breakfasts I can get from one baggie of Granola. Also, I don't seem to need to eat as much while I'm hiking as I do when I'm engaged in more sedentary enterprises.

Right now the trail climbs again, gently, much unlike the switchback agony of yesterday's ascents and descents, out of that infernal basin. There'll never be a shortage of mosquitoes. Oops. Their break must be over. I was just thinking how nice it was to be away from their whiny little plague when one drilled right through my sock.

I must be getting in shape. Even walking tiptoe on my left foot, I seem to be putting the trail behind me faster than the day.

1:43 p.m.

My feet are screaming for a rest. These thin-soled Nikes don't blister or squeeze or smash my feet as the boots do, but they bruise the bottoms of my feet, because through their soles I feel every little rock, every countour line—like where the horse stepped in the mud a month ago and his shoe print is baked in the path today. This is like walking 45-50 miles wearing bedroom slippers.

Little frogs hop across my path. I greet them: "Eat lots of mosquitoes." They pause to consider this, then hop along, intent on their business.

Flathead Indians believed there was a frog in the moon. She's still there. I saw her last night.

In those days the world was dark, because there was no sun. The people were convinced that their wickedness was caused by the darkness, so they held a convention to figure out how to enlighten the world. Only Sinchlep (We know him as Coyote.) was able to figure out how to bring the light.

This light of Sinchlep's was a little bit less than the sun, and the people were very happy to have it, but Sinchlep got into trouble while performing his new duties. The people of that time could speak, and Sinchlep, coming round each day with his light, could see what the people did. Sometimes the people, who were used to darkness, did things they wished to remain private. Sinchlep, however, published whatever gossip he gathered as he accompanied the light on its rounds. The people, being very angry, grabbed Sinchlep by the tail, which was then very long, and threw him to the ground, preventing him from being the sun any more.

The crow then offered to take the place of Sinchlep, but, he gave very little light because he was so black. The people laughed at him and pointed and he could not stand their ridicule, so he retired.

Finally Amotkan (whose name in the later years of the tribe evolved to mean President of the United States) sent one of his sons, Spokani, to enlighten the world. Spokani wished to marry a woman of the earth before ascending into the sky, but when he came down from the heavens and landed in a camp of the Flatheads, the people were afraid and would not admit him to their lodges.

Unhappy, he headed off toward the river, where he met a family of frogs. To them he complained of his treatment by the Flatheads and told them that he desired, therefore, to marry a frog. One large, fat frog literally jumped at the chance. She jumped up and smacked him on the cheek, where she became a lump on his cheek. The marriage was thus consummated.

The people were furious to see the handsome Spokani disfigured, so they tried to kill the frog by beating her with sticks. She cried in pain and shame and pleaded with her husband to leave the earth. He immediately rose above the earth. To revenge himself on the people for their contempt, he does not allow them to see him clearly during the day, when he dresses himself in shimmering robes and crosses the waters under the earth. He can still be seen, though, in the night sky, with his wife the frog on his cheek.[5]

For the past hour or so I've been walking through a lovely

hemlock and fir forest of huge trees, wide-spaced like a park, interspersed with pristine, grassy meadows. No mosquitoes. If heaven ain't a lot like Oregon, I don't want to go.

Down to my last quart of water again. I'll have to make it to Stuart Falls tonight.

Day 6—June 27, 1987—Mazama Campground, Crater Lake National Park:

When I got to Stuart Falls, I decided to keep on walking. Not far up a very steep trail the trees were spangled with boundary signs. Half a mile later a sign announced that I was entering Crater Lake National Park, that it was 8.8 miles to Mazama Campground. It was 5 p.m. and 8.8 miles seemed quite a stretch, but I decided to go until I felt like quitting. As always, the mosquitoes were a factor in the decision, making even hesitation along the trail an unbearable ordeal. Crater Lake is just a huge, leaky holding tank and the seeps and springs abounding on its edges make an environment as attractive to mosquitoes as either of the lake basins in the Sky Lakes Wilderness. Soon they were out in clouds again and I was churning along the trail in long pants and hooded sweatshirt with the hood up.

Somewhere near here, so the legend goes, is the Lost Cabin Mine. In fact, it was a search for the mine that led to the discovery of Crater Lake:

Back in the winter of 1850-51 a prospector staggered into a saloon in Yreka and shouted "Set 'em up! Drinks for the house, on me." Up in Oregon, he said, he'd struck it rich, built a little cabin, worked his mine all summer and fall, and he'd come to winter in Yreka and have a good time. "Set 'em up!" he shouted again, and again drinks were poured all around. He shouted "Set 'em up!" so many times that winter that folks around Yreka began to call him Set 'em Up.

In the spring of 1851, Set 'em Up disappeared. He was

gone all summer, but he reappeared late in the fall and spent the winter of 1851-52 setting 'em up again in Yreka's saloons. No one was surprised when spring rolled around and Set 'em Up was gone once again, but when he failed to return for the winter of 1852-53, he was sorely missed, especially by his drinking buddies, who had grown to depend upon his generosity. As the winter wore on, speculation about when Set 'em Up would arrive turned to resignation that there would be fewer free drinks in Yreka that winter, and then to speculation about Set 'em Up's claim.

Set 'em Up was vague when it came to the particulars of his mine, but, over the course of many dreary, boozy evenings, he leaked enough information across the barroom tables to inspire much confident speculation, not only about its location, but about its size. All agreed that the mine, which was by then known as the Lost Cabin Mine, was big—a regular Eldorado—and everyone knew that the mine was close to his cabin. "Find the cabin, and you've found the mine."

Night after night, the Lost Cabin Mine was discussed, debated, and deliberated. If something happened to Set 'em Up—and something surely must have happened to him, else he'd be in Yreka right now, setting 'em up—the gold belonged to no one. It was there for the taking and there was something, well, something unChristian about ignoring free money. And who—they demanded—who had more right—no—more of an obligation to carry on Set 'em Up's work than those folks who befriended him these last two winters? No one, of course. When the warm winds of spring blew through Yreka in 1853, the decision was made: eleven Yreka miners would go to Oregon to search for the Lost Cabin Mine.

In May, as the snow receded high into the Cascades, the Californians reached the outskirts of Jacksonville. So they wouldn't attract attention, they camped outside town and sent a couple of their members in for supplies. Jacksonville's saloons were as attractive as those in Yreka, though, and one of the Californians found himself sharing a bottle and conversation with a friendly Jacksonville prospector. Even in Jacksonville they'd heard of the Lost Cabin Mine and the Californian, his lips loosened by whiskey, soon let the word out: They'd come to search for the Lost Cabin Mine. Not only that, but their leader, a good friend of old Set 'em Up, heard from Set 'em Up himself enough information about the location of the mine that they were sure to find it.

The Californian was barely out of the saloon before eleven Jacksonville prospectors were hot on his trail. J. W. Hillman was one of the Jacksonville eleven:

...We made quick preparations, got some provisions together, and started after the California miners, who soon discovered we were on their trail; and then it was a game of hide-and-seek, until rations on both sides began to get low.

The Californians would push through the brush, scatter, double backwards on their trail, and then camp in the most inaccessible places to be found, and it sometimes puzzled us to locate and camp near enough to watch them. One day while thus engaged, and when provisions had run very low, each party scattered out to look for anything in the shape of game that could be found. On my return from an unsuccessful hunt, I passed close to the camp of the Californians. Up to this time neither party had spoken to one of the others, but, seeing a young fellow in camp, I bade him good day, and got in conversation with him. He asked me what our object was in the mountains and why we hung so close to their trail.

I frankly told him we believed their leader had certain landmarks, which, if found, would enable them to locate the Lost Cabin, and as we were all pretty good prospectors and hunters, we intended to stay with them until the mine was found or starvation drove us back to the valley. After this a truce was declared, and we worked and hunted in unison. One day, just before deciding that it was no longer safe to stay in the mountains with our very limited supply of food and no game to be found, we camped on the side of a mountain, and after consultation it was decided that a few of each party should take what provisions could be spared, and for a couple of days longer hunt for landmarks which the leader of the California party was in search of; of that party I was one...

On the evening of the first day, while riding up a long, sloping mountain, we suddenly came in sight of water, and were very much surprised, as we did not expect to see any lakes, and did not know but what we had come in sight of and close to Klamath Lake, and not until my mule stopped within a few feet of the rim of Crater Lake did I look down, and if I had been riding a blind mule I firmly believe I would have ridden over the edge to death and destruction.

Every man of the party gazed with wonder at the sight before him, and each in his own peculiar way gave expression to the thoughts within him; but we had no time to lose, and after rolling some boulders down the side of the lake, we rode to the left, as near the rim as possible, past the butte, looking to see an outlet for the lake, but we could find none.

I was very anxious to find a way to the water, which was immediately vetoed by the whole party, and as the leader of the Californians had become discouraged, we decided to return to camp; but not before we discussed what name we should give the lake. There were many names suggested, but Mysterious Lake and Deep Blue Lake were most favorably received, and on a vote, Deep Blue Lake was chosen for a name.

We secured a small stick, about the size of a walking cane, and with a knife made a slit in one end. A piece of paper was torn from a memorandum book, our names written on it, the paper stuck in the slit, and the stick propped up in the ground to the best of our ability. We then reluctantly turned our backs upon the future Crater Lake of Oregon.

The finding of Crater Lake was an accident, as we were not looking for lakes; but the fact of my being the first upon its banks was due to the fact that I was riding the best saddle mule in southern

Oregon, the property of Jimmy Dobson, a miner and packer, with headquarters at Jacksonville, who had furnished me the mule in consideration of a claim to be taken in his name should we be successful.

Stranger to me than our discovery was the fact that after our return I could get no acknowledgment from any Indian, buck or squaw, old or young, that any such lake existed; each and every one denied any knowledge of it, or ignored the subject completely.[6]

It was no wonder the Indians wouldn't talk about it. To them, Crater Lake was an evil pit, and to look upon it or even to speak about it was forbidden. Oliver Cromwell Applegate got the story, though, and wrote it down for his friend Robert Miller of Jacksonville in 1882. I found the letter in a scrapbook in the Oregon Collection at the University of Oregon Library. "It is a sadly disconnected story," he says, his ink pen flowing across the narrow stationery, "but you may have the priviledge of changing the wording in any place you may see fit." I've changed it a little, but here, essentially, is the story he told Miller:

Crater Lake was once ruled by a beautiful witch called La-o, who lived with her servants and pets in a large, lovely house on an island in the middle of the lake. In those days the lake was shallow, like a pond, and filled with lovely flowers and exotic fish. A bright fire blazed always in La-o's house, so that it was always warm and comfortable and inviting.

La-o wandered the countryside, winning men's hearts. She lurked near watering places where, disguised as a beautiful woman, she met men who invited her into their lodges. In return, she invited them to her home on the island, an invitation no man could refuse. Once on the island, her visitors were killed and, except for their hearts, eaten by La-o's servants and pets. The hearts were hung up to dry and were later used as balls in games played by invited guests. Though everyone knew La-o by reputation, she had so many clever disguises that she was never recognized until it was too late.

One man, however, was impervious to La-o's charm. His name was Skell and he lived with his mother and brother over in the Yamsi country. Skell seldom traveled, but he knew everything. La-o came, one afternoon, to the spring near Skell's house, but Skell knew why she had come and he refused to go out of his house to meet her.

La-o was not to be denied. She entered the house and asked Skell to come with her to her home on the island. Skell did not answer. Furious, she leapt on him, pinned his arms to his side and carried him away. Skell struggled, but he was no match for the powerful La-o.

After she had carried him for a long distance, Skell knew they were nearing La-o's house. "My head itches," he told her. "Please let go of my arm so that I may scratch my head."

"You won't live long enough to suffer," La-o cackled, but she let go of one arm so he could scratch his head. In one smooth motion, Skell drew a knife from his hair and sliced La-o's throat.

Skell dragged La-o's body to the edge of the lake and carved it into twelve pieces. Then he called to La-o's servants, "Here is Skell's flesh," and he began to throw the pieces over the edge toward La-o's house. The servants were hungry, so they eagerly caught the pieces of flesh and gobbled them down. Skell kept Lao's head until the rest of the flesh had been eaten and then, shouting "Here is Lao's head," he threw it into the lake.

Realizing Skell's hideous trick, the servants were furious. Skell ran toward his home with the servants hot on his heels. He'd not gone far when he met his brother coming down the trail, carrying Skell's magic cane. Skell drew a line across the trail with the cane, through which a stream suddenly flowed. The servants dived in and began swimming across. Skell ran for home.

Skell's wife stood guard at the door, her dagger ready for the attack. When the first of La-o's servants appeared, she stabbed at him and missed and then chased him around the house. With the door unguarded, the rest of La-o's servants were able to rush into the house, overpower Skell, and carry him to La-o's house where they killed him and ate all but his heart, which was hung up to dry.

Though it was unknown to La-o, one of her servants was a friend of Skell's. After he was killed, this servant found a lock of his hair. He took it to Skell's uncle, a great spirit, who steamed it in a large pot and caused Skell to reappear. When La-o's servants heard of Skell's reappearance, they went to his home to kill him. Skell's wife saw them coming, and she vanished into the fog. They rushed into the house once again and struck simultaneously with their daggers. Because he was now a spirit with no heart, Skell vanished.

La-o's half-sister, Chilock, took possession of the house and the lake. La-o's spirit often visited Chilock. The spirit did not want the people to know that she had been killed. She wanted them to think that she had bewitched Skell and taken his heart, so she asked Chilock to invite all her friends over to play the game in which they used the hearts.

On the day of the game, Chilock heard beautiful singing. She investigated and found an old woman, very dirty and poorly dressed. Though she did not know it, this was Skell's uncle, the great spirit, in disguise.

Soon the guests arrived and took their places for the game. The old woman sang her chanting songs and when the game began, she asked for Skell's heart. Chilock gave her a heart and told her it was Skell's, but the heart was old and dry and the old woman knew it was not Skell's. She knew Skell's heart would be fresh. Again and again she asked for Skell's heart, and again and again Chilock substituted a different heart. Finally Chilock was so charmed by the old woman's songs that she forgot what she was doing and gave her Skell's heart.

Skell's brother had hired the swiftest animals and birds to steal the heart from the players as it passed the lower end of the grassy field where the game was being played. The antelope grabbed it first and passed it to the dove who carried it to Skell's brother. He passed it to Skell's uncle, who shed his disguise and became again the great spirit. Skell's uncle steamed the heart as he had the lock of hair, and Skell lived again.

Skell's uncle knew that the spirit of La-o continued to inhabit the lake. To make sure that it and the evil retinue stayed in one place, "He caused sword-like knives to be placed all around the lake so close together that nothing could get through them. He then caused the bottom of the lake to fall to a great depth and the home of La-o to sink into the deep water. Her house was ruined and her fire extinguished. He changed the servants into hideous reptiles and fierce animals and called the place *Gka was* (Home of Evil Spirits). The spirit of La-o was there and presided over all and it was immediate death to anyone who should look on the lake. If anyone ate near the place the food would become poison and kill them..." Because the monsters would not eat the head of La-o, it remains there today. We call it Wizard Island.[7]

5.4 miles from the park boundary I hit highway 62, a couple of miles from the campground, making about 25 miles for the day. A half mile or so up the road a Vietnamese couple with four little children, traveling in a broken down VW bus, were about to be towed away by a AAA wrecker. I asked the wrecker driver for a lift and so finished my trip through the wilderness atop a tool box on the back of a wrecker.

I called home and Chris said she would pick me up at nine or so this morning. I put up the tent for the second time on this trip, as the mosquitoes were still finding me irresistible, cooked a Cupasoup and a cup of tea in the dark and then went to bed, expecting to fall asleep immediately. My feet hurt so bad...

Spring, 1989, and still I dream of hiking the whole route. Last summer I hiked, with Chris, another 100 miles, from Willamette Pass to Santiam Pass. This summer I'll hike another hundred or so. I'll just keep moving till I make it.

Stephen Meek, pictured here, agreed to "pilot the company safely through in thirty days, or, as was written in his own words, give his head for a football." (Photo courtesy of Oregon Historical Society)

Along the
Terrible Trail

...a fine gentleman by the name of Stephen Meek encouraged the company to take a new route with him for the pilot.

I was much opposed to it but the company would go and I went also and found an awful road, sometimes without grass or water, and were fifteen days later than the companies that took the old road. However we got through safe, with a good deal of suffering on the part of some for want of provisions and a good many deaths when we got to the Mission where we took water.

From H. D. Martin, in a letter from Yam Hill, Oregon Territory, appearing in <u>The Gazette,</u> *St. Joseph, Mo., Aug. 21, 1846*

Our emigration of 1845 would have gotten down in good time as a part did, if they had not been led astray by a pilot by the name of Stephen Meeks who undertook to pilot what was called the St. Joseph Company consisting of 214 wagons, a nearer route from Big Snake river to the Dalls on the Columbia.

They were out near 40 days longer than they should have been if they had kept on the old road. They run out of provisions and then had to eat their poor cattle, which gave them a camp fever and were out of water 12 to 24 hours and had not sufficient for the sick or children which gave them intense suffering, and the loss of near 50 souls, old and young.

The greatest number that died were children...Those that

The Meek Cutoff, Oregon's Terrible Trail 1845

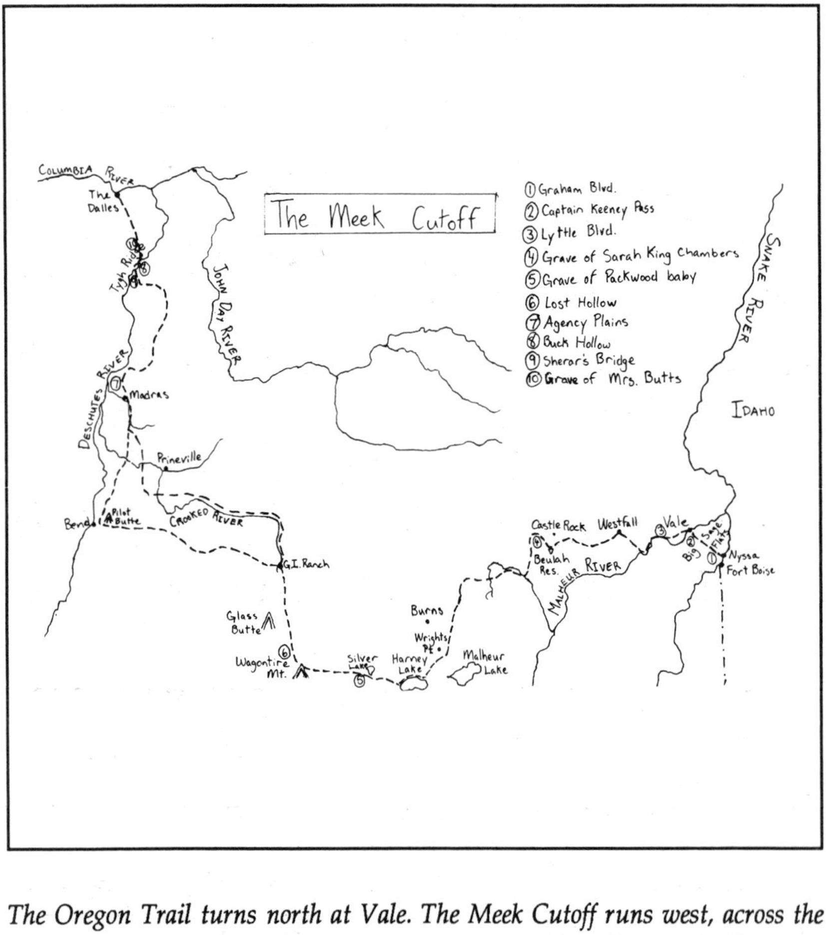
The Meek Cutoff
① Graham Blvd.
② Captain Keeney Pass
③ Lyttle Blvd.
④ Grave of Sarah King Chambers
⑤ Grave of Packwood baby
⑥ Lost Hollow
⑦ Agency Plains
⑧ Buck Hollow
⑨ Sherar's Bridge
⑩ Grave of Mrs. Butts
COLUMBIA RIVER
The Dalles
Tygh Ridge
JOHN DAY RIVER
DESCHUTES RIVER
Madras
Prineville
CROOKED RIVER
Bend
Pilot Butte
G.I. Ranch
Glass Butte
Wagontire Mt.
Silver Lake
Harney Lake
Burns
Wrights Pt.
Malheur Lake
Castle Rock
Westfall
Vale
Beulah Res.
MALHEUR RIVER
Big Sage Flat
Nyssa
Fort Boise
SNAKE RIVER
IDAHO

The Oregon Trail turns north at Vale. The Meek Cutoff runs west, across the Oregon Desert. Expecting a shorter, easier route to the Willamette Valley, more than 1000 people attempted the Meek Cutoff in August, 1845. Approximately 50 people died before the survivors reached The Dalles.

traveled the old road got in well and in good time."
> *From Hiram Smith, in a letter*
> *appearing in* The Gazette,
> *St. Joseph, Missouri,*
> *Friday, July 17, 1846*

August 23, 1845

Went four miles this morning, which took us to Fort Boise, which stands on the eastern bank of Snake River near the mouth of the Boise. It is a small, mean-looking fort, built like the others of sun-dried mud moulded into the shape of bricks, and appears more calculated for the collection of furs from other forts than for trading in its own immediate vicinity, as there is no game there, and the Indians living in this part of the country are very poor, many of them nearly naked and living on fish and roots.

It is necessary to re-cross Snake river at this place, which is here fordable and we all got safely over during the afternoon, camping on the western bank. The indians assisted us in crossing, showing us the ford and helping us to drive the loose cattle, in return for which a few presents pleased them greatly. The river is near half a mile wide, and so deep as to run over the tops of the wagon sides in places, but as it was generally of uniform depth all the way across, the current was not so rapid as at the other crossing.

> *James Field*

I stood with my heels on the Idaho border and looked west into the darkness. Earlier that day I stashed my Jeep in Burns and took the Greyhound to Nyssa, arriving at 1 a.m. Now it was nearly two and I'd got my bearings and was headed out of town.

My companions, ghosts all, came to Oregon in 1845, members of the largest wagon train yet to cross the continent. They followed the Oregon Trail (which they refer to as the "old road") until they arrived at Vale. There the Oregon Trail turns north to pass through the Blue Mountains on its way to the

Columbia River. From Vale they traveled a different route, the Meek Cut-off, which meanders west across the desert to Bend and then north to The Dalles. In my dreams of this trip, the Snake was wild, and Oregon lay before me like a smorgasbord of wilderness delights.

Stephen Meek, who guided the wagon train across the plains, believed he could save time and avoid hostile Indians who were thought to lurk in the Blue Mountains by continuing to drive west. He passed through that country several years earlier on a trapping expedition and believed that he could again find water and grass in abundance. Nearly two hundred families followed his lead, straight west across the desert.

William Helm and Samuel Parker were married men. Jesse Harritt and James Field were single. Helm, a Methodist preacher whose considerable family and their belongings traveled to Oregon in two blue wagons, chaired the meetings called to write the constitution of the 70-wagon Savannah Oregon Emigrating Society and, with Solomon Tetherow, Lewis Thompson, Zachariah Moorland and James Officer, was a member of the committee formed to draft laws and regulations for the journey.

Harritt, Field and Parker left, in their journals, records of their passage over the Meek Cutoff. William Helm left no journal, but others wrote about him, so we know more about him than the others at the outset of the journey. Harritt, Field, and Parker we come to know gradually, through their journals, as the emigration progresses.

The "CONSTITUTION LAWS &C", among other things, defined the duties and method of selection of the officers of the Society, and required the "necessary outfit to consist of 150 lbs of flour or 100 lbs of flour and 75 pounds of meal and 50 lbs of bacon per every person in the company excepting infants..." Murderers and stray dogs were to be punished by death. "Any one guilty of rape or attempt at it..." received 39 lashes per day for three days "on their bare back." Those guilty of larceny, fornication, or open adultery received 39 lashes on the bare back. In addition, larcenists were fined "double the amount". "Anyone guilty of indecent language" would be fined, "at the discretion of the Ex. Council."

"My father would not join a train whose members planned to travel on Sunday," R. W. Helm told Fred Lockley in 1924. "He circulated around among the emigrants and quietly organized a group of men who were willing to lay over on Sundays...They overtook many of the other emigrants who had nearly run the legs off their oxen by traveling hard and fast and not giving their oxen a chance to rest up on Sundays." Members of the Savannah Oregon Emigrating Society contributed 25 cents each to purchase a large tent in which William Helm preached every Sunday morning and evening during the emigration.

The Helm family, according to the Census of the Oregon Emigration, consisted of 9 persons total—3 armed men, one female under 14, one female over 14, and four males under 16. In their two blue wagons they carried no meat—intending, I imagine, to eat what they could shoot, or butcher their loose cattle as needed—1400 pounds of flour, 450 pounds of bacon, 6 pounds of powder and 20 pounds of lead. John W. Helm, was listed as a cattle driver responsible for 18 head of loose cattle, 12 oxen, one mule or horse, and three guns or pistols. George Waulor Helm and William Helm were included in the Role of Armed Men.

William Helm was 45 years old in 1845. I am 47 in 1989, so, we travel the Cutoff as contemporaries, though 144 years separate our journeys.

Back in 1845, the Snake was wild, but the river I heard that night flowed along with barely a ripple, gently lapping the shore, tamed by dams and irrigation projects, domestic now as an old dog. My Oregon Trail was paved and straight, a precise gridwork of roads laid down with a ruler on a map to run efficiently through an agri-factory of plowed, leveled and irrigated fields.

August 22, 1845

Crosed the Snake River Verry deep

Samuel Parker

"Hey. Wait. Esscuse me." Two winos cuddled a jug on a bench beneath a big green traffic sign. One heaved himself to his feet and staggered across the street toward me. He was about my height and nearly as bulky. He wore army fatigues and approached me with his hand upraised. In the shadows cast by the streetlight he looked sinister, threatening. I turned to face him.

"Esscuse me," he said again. "What way is Vale?"

I pointed to the big green traffic sign beneath which he and his friend had been sitting. "That way."

"Oh." He seemed disappointed. "We need to go to Vale."

"That's the way," I told him.

"Oh," he said again. "Where you goin'?"

"To the home of a friend, over there," I lied, waving vaguely toward some houses down the road in front of me.

"Okaaay. Thank you," he said thickly, and staggered back across the street. I hiked on down the road, following a different route to Vale, stopping frequently to look back.

I hiked south, paralleling the Snake River, looking for Lytle Boulevard, which follows the Oregon Trail up East Cow Canyon, through Captain Keeney Pass and down to the Malheur River and Vale. But that was for tomorrow. My plans for the rest of that night were to find a place to sleep until the sun rose.

I walked on through the night. Nyssa was behind me but every farmhouse, barnyard, cattle pen, irrigation pump, road intersection and power pole seemed to have its own mercury vapor light, so my walk through the desert night was illuminated, mile after mile, like street corners in Portland. It's odd to me that folks would live in a country place with clear air and a star-spangled sky and then spend their nights in the glare of these awful lights. If I lived here one of the first things I'd do is shoot out all the mercury vapor lights so my neighbors and I could have an uninterrupted view of the sky. I should have shot out a few that night, but it was late and I was tired, so I pressed on.

Three a.m. and still I walk. A cow, startled by this apparition staggering out of the night, snorts and bawls and thunders from the fence. A farm dog barks his mates awake. Together they warn me to keep moving. A horse nickers and trots to the edge of my vision where he becomes a shadow with shiny eyes. In a pool of light up the road a white cat eyes me suspiciously and then slinks up a driveway and disappears beneath a truck. Always water runs, rushes, down the ditches flanking the road, through culverts beneath it, an aural backdrop against which the night is played out. In my ear a mosquito whines. ("They carry AIDS, you know," the attendant at the Burns gas/bus station told me authoritatively, as he sprayed my bare legs with mosquito repellent.) Irrigation ditches everywhere, and mile after mile of fields preened and powdered and furrowed, but no place for the weary traveler to throw his sleeping bag.

At last, a little grove of willows. It lies between two farmyards, just far enough from each that it's on the edge of the mercury vapor glare. I hopped the ditch at the edge of the road and burrowed into the brush, flushing a covey of birds—quail, maybe—that fluttered off, complaining, into the night. No one else complained, so I dug out my sleeping bag and, as soon as I lay down, was sound asleep.

August 23, 1845

"Went to Malhune Creek 16"

Samuel Parker

June 26, 1989, 7:26 a.m.

A baby meadowlark preens his feathers on a branch above my head when I awake. Mourning doves I hear, and sparrows, and the raucous challenge of a cock pheasant. A quail sits on a fence post not far away and, of course, cattle bawl in the distance. A New Holland swather wheezes by just across the ditch. Its driver doesn't see me.

I dig out my little butane stove and brew a cup of coffee. Soon, my heart ticks again. I face the sun and contemplate my surroundings. The quarter acre of willows and brush in which I slept is apparently the only wild patch of ground around. Across the road, downhill to the east, carefully tilled fields stretch to the Snake River. Two, perhaps three, miles away to the west, a line of sagebrush marks the edge of the cropland. The vast fields are without clods, the soil worked and re-worked into fine powder, then leveled and furrowed and seeded.

Saddle up. As usual, my pack is far too heavy and as I struggled into its harness an inventory of excess gear races through my mind. How little we really need. I'll sort it out in Vale, mail the excess to myself in Burns, pick it up when I get there, pack it into the Jeep. Already my legs are tired. I'm not as fit as I should be. But then, I never am.

A big Jersey cow lay dead next to a tractor at the edge of the road about a hundred yards away. Behind her, a white board fence, lush green grass and shade trees surround a big white farmhouse. On the blacktop near the cow, two boys dribble and shoot at a basket hung from a power pole. Three men in white straw hats and snap-button shirts stand near the cow.

"Hi. How are you doing?"
"Fine, thanks."

June 26, 1989 (continued)
Stopped for breakfast along a canal that intersects the Oregon Trail. I am proceeding at approximately two miles per hour. Legs tired. A flock of magpies filled the air with squawks and wings when I sat down. Blackbirds and redwinged black-birds and a flock of Canada geese keep me company this morning. I am on the edge of the sagebrush and relieved to have the agrifactory behind me.

I hike on. Soon the the water disappears, sucked into a giant siphon, shot beneath Lytle Boulevard and then released into a canal high on the other side.

Lytle Boulevard, a paved country road with a city name, is the Oregon Trail. Except for the pavement, this is familiar ground for my companions. They recall the sagebrush (They called it wormwood.), the lay of the land uphill to Captain Keeney Pass (though the pass was nameless in their day) and even the ruts that still remain from the passing of their wagons. They also recall rumors of trouble awaiting them along the Old Road:

August 24, 1845
The story of the murder of two Frenchmen is pronounced a humbug by the people at the Fort. They say that the Walla Wallas entertain a hostile feeling towards us, and will probably try to injure us as we pass through their territory, but their numbers or equipments would not render them dangerous to such sized companies as we are in at present. Still, the nature of the country is such that if they took advantage of it they could damage us considerably.

A man named Meek has engaged to pilot the leading company, Capt. Owensby's, which is the only one now ahead of us. He was to guide the outfit through to the Dalles of the Columbia river by

a new, and near route, following the pack trail from Fort Boise and missing the Walla Wallas altogether, leaving Fort Walla Walla on his right and cutting off between 100 and 200 miles of travel. A vote was take whether we should follow them or keep the old way, and a majority decided upon the new one. We traveled about 16 miles, camping upon Malheur creek near the forks of the two roads.
James Field

So I trudged on, northeast up Lytle Boulevard, around Lincoln Bench, up East Cow Hollow toward Vale. The canal flows southeast. In a couple of miles East Cow Hollow branched off to the left, but the Oregon Trail winds upward to Captain Keeney Pass. Along the road, markers like concrete fence posts show the route of the Oregon Trail, climbing up the gulley bottom.

Near the top of the hill, ruts, gouged by thousands of wagon wheels and widened and deepened by nearly 144 years of erosion, testify to the passage of the immigrants. Ghosts are thick here. I hike down off the Boulevard and walk a hundred feet or so between the ruts. The soil is dry, soft and dusty, beneath my feet. A little green remains in the grass, but it, too, is mostly dry and brittle.

The wagons passed over this very spot. Bachelors Harritt and Field walked here and today, in my mind, they walk here again, bullwhackers, probably, urging burdened beasts over the endless hills. Helm and Parker were taciturn family men accompanied by wives and children. They, too, probably walked alongside their wagons, urging their oxen ever westward.

Photography wasn't invented until 1839, so pictures of this generation are fairly rare, but when I looked through the collection of photographs at the Oregon Historical Society I was struck by how strong the men and women who came to Oregon in the 1840s looked. As a group, they lacked beauty.

Indeed, they weren't even handsome. They had in common, though, an expression of confidence and determination borne on high, bony brows, and prominent jaws. There were no bald men. Their eyes were sharp and focused, and they seemed to dare the photographer to pull off this modern scientific miracle of photography. With their hard, angular, rational faces posed for the camera, they looked sceptical, capable, and tough.

The round faces and prematurely bald heads of their grandchildren, with whom they share the photo files, affirm that the pioneers found the promised land, but suggest that its blessings might have been mixed. These, too, are people of accomplishment, successful people—chairman of this or that important committee, heads of corporations, mayors of Oregon's towns—but where their fathers and mothers were all angles, bones, hardness, their citified, domestic offspring were pure pudgy softness. The pioneers seemed to have been the color of saddle leather; their children, shaven and bathed, were pink. Their brows, cheekbones, and jaws lay buried beneath the bounty of too much food. Multiple chins, boiled-looking skin, unfocused eyes, capillaries broadened by alcohol—the soft living sought by our grandfathers had unintended consequences for their children.

> *August 25, 1845*
> *Since crossing to this side of Snake River again the road has been fearfully dusty. In fact, a person who has never traveled these wormwood barrens can form no idea as to what depth dust may be cut up in them by a few wagons passing. To a person walking in the road it is frequently more than shoe deep, and if the wind happens to blow lengthwise with the road, it raises such a fog you cannot see the wagon next in front.*
>
> *James Field*

Right. Sorry, James. I drifted back to the present for a

moment.

So I sit between the ruts of the Oregon Trail, and see you and your westering clan climb this hill. Fifty or 60 wagons stretch from here around that bend. The wind lifts the shouts of bullwhackers, the creak of harness leather, and the laughter of little children and carries them to my ears. Somewhere a camp dog yips, horses nicker, and oxen bellow in protest as the hill steepens near the crest. And the dust. Always the dust, and the smell of sage, borne away on the wind as wheel after wheel churns the earth. Almost to the top now...

"Hey...what are you doing? Are you a geol...?" Wind carries the words away.

The stern old pioneer stares across the years at me. How do I explain? I sit in the center of the Oregon Trail, no doubt square in front of his ox team. His stolid, impassive stare asks without asking: *"What manner of man is this? Daydreaming when there's work to be done, his butt planted firmly in the way of my wagon..."*

"Sorry, Grandfather. I'm a writer..." I start to explain. His expression doesn't change.

"Holy God, Martha, a writer." Martha Scroggins Helm, my five-times-great grandmother, sits in the blue covered wagon, reins in hand, waiting for this 20th century impediment to move out of the way. *"Older than I am and he's a teller of tales, a day-dreamer."*

"Hey. What are you doing? Are you a geologist?"

A geologist? There's a thought. "No. Not a geologist. A writer," I explain again.

"Are you okay?" A big sunburned hand grasps my shoulder. For the first time I notice heat waves rising from the sand. Four pair of scuffed cowboy boots stand in a neat circle around me. The hand on my shoulder is attached to an equally big sunburned arm.

"Oh, yeah. I'm okay." Where'd these people come from?

"Must have just dozed off or something." Over on Lytle Boulevard an old Ford pickup idles, glinting in the sunlight, its doors agape. As I struggled to regain my feet, another large hand grabbed my arm and lifted, gently helping me up. "Thanks."

"I've already claimed all this land around here, far as you can see on both sides of the road. Who you working for?"

He was big, big as a barn, big as a Hereford bull, which he resembled. A sweat-stained red baseball cap with "Diesel Power" stitched across its front sat uneasily atop his head, a little baseball bird in a tangled nest of red-gray hair. He wore faded Levis and a t-shirt but the most remarkable thing about him was his belly. Covered in reddish fir, punctuated with a scar from some old knife fight that worked in concert with his belly button to form an exclamation point, it struggled out of his Levis, liberated in a gap between his tortured t-shirt and low-slung jeans. Cold blue eyes, just slits, really, against the desert sun, peered down at me from just above a bushy red beard.

"Some son of a bitch's been out here staking claims on land I already claimed," he growled. "Now I have to go around and restake my claims. Makes a hell of a lot of work."

His companions, two young men and a girl, were small and dark, burnished, not burned, by the sun and wind. Slim and fit, all bone and sinew, they stood aloof on long legs made for hiking, looking me over in silence. "So who are you working for?" he demanded again.

"Just working for myself right now." I told them of the 1845 wagon train, of my night-time hike through the desert, that I hoped to make it to Vale by evening.

"You sure you're all right?" He shook his big head in amazement. "Walking around out here in this heat..." his voice trailed off. "This sun'll kill you, you know. We can give you a ride into Vale."

I thanked him but declined the ride. They turned and walked back up the hill toward the road. "If you see any geologists or prospectors out here you tell 'em—I already claimed this land," he shouted from the top of the ditchbank. Then they climbed into the pickup cab and roared up the hill toward Captain Keeney Pass.

I looked again across the desert. White PVC claimstakes sprouted among the sagebrush like water pipes awaiting sprinklerheads. A gold rush was underway, right here beneath my nose.

I imagined an army of colorful, offbeat characters in floppy hats armed with picks and shovels and gold pans, riding faithful mules or puttering through the sagebrush in beat-up Jeeps, picking, burrowing in the desert floor and panning along the banks of the infrequent desert streams, looking for the mother lode. Dangerous Dan McGrew was there—I think I just met him—and Sam McGee, and the lady that's known as Lou. But hold on there, Pardner. That was yesterday.

I should have imagined roads like scars criss-crossing the delicate desert terrain and powerful, smoke-belching machines shattering the gentle desert silence. I should have imagined plastic-lined ponds, filled with liquid cyanide, and heaps of cyanide-laced tailings that remain for centuries, the desert's new skyline.

I should have imagined the deer and the antelope, dead. I should have imagined dead ducks and geese, dead meadowlarks, sparrows, robins, owls, hawks, dead coyotes, cottontails, cattle, packrats. And what of the vulture, riding gently on the updrafts, and the magpie in his elegant natural tuxedo, and the others who come to feast on the carrion bounty? And the rattlesnake and lizard? Yes, them, too. Dead. The desert, dead.

And the pits—godawful, mind-boggling, desert-destroying pits—blasted, scraped, gouged a thousand or so feet into the heart of the desert, thousands of acres across. I should have imagined the pits.

Low-grade deposits like those in the Oregon desert cannot be mined profitably by that colorful crew with their picks and shovels. Open pit mining and cyanide heap leaching bring technology to bear on the problem of profitably removing minute particles of gold from enormous quantities of ore. The residual effects of these operations are an environmentalist's nightmare.

In an open pit mine, low-grade ore is dredged and trucked from an ever-deepening and ever-widening pit to outdoor heaps. An irrigation system sprinkles the ore heaps with a cyanide solution, which trickles through the ore, leaching away gold and silver particles. The solution collects in plastic-lined ponds, is filtered to remove the precious metals, and then recycled to begin again its treasure-collecting journey.

Cyanide, a deadly poison, is an immediate threat to wildlife and cattle. Miners may cover cyanide-filled storage ponds with heavy plastic nets and surround them with fences, but a thirsty animal seeking water in a desert will find a way to it. When a cyanide pond leaks, as it did at a Nevada mine in 1989, the poison will find a way into the groundwater. In Nevada, for instance, since 1984, when the Nevada Department of Wildlife instituted a voluntary reporting regulation, cyanide mining companies have reported the deaths of 6213 animals, "mostly migratory birds and mostly as a result of exposure to cyanide-laced ponds."[1]

Open-pit mines typically operate for a few years, until the ore plays out, and then close down. Mining companies move on, but the pits, some of which are more than a thousand feet deep and broad enough to swallow a small city, remain, as do small mountains of cyanide-laced tailings.

Seventy percent of Malheur County is federal land,

administered by the BLM. (In the American southwest these initials are thought to stand for Bureau of Livestock and Mining. In the northwest the agency is known more for its slavish adherence to the demands of the timber industry and is therefore known as the Bureau of Lumber and Mining.)

There are now no federal or state regulations requiring mining companies to return the landscape to its original condition. Though the BLM happily ignores environmental regulations and even the recommendations of its own biologists when there's an "overriding need to sell timber"[2] or overgraze, or build roads, or spray herbicides, or mine precious minerals—any activity that promotes the welfare of the industries this agency was invented to serve—it operates best in a regulation vacuum like the one now existing in Oregon. Relying on the BLM to protect southeastern Oregon's fragile desert environment in the midst of a cyanide heap-leach mining stampede is asking the fox to guard the henhouse.

Oregon has already been burned once, in Baker County. The "...operators of the Minexco mine went out of business in the mid-1980s, failed to reclaim the land and to detoxify concentrated cyanide on the site..."[3]

Mining companies are not philanthropies. Unless required to do so, they won't reclaim a devastated environment. The BLM exists to serve extractive industries, not to require responsible environmental management. The prospect of an Oregon desert landscape permanently pocked by huge pits and pimpled with piles of poisonous tailings is frighteningly real.

"*Pocked. Pimpled. Poisoned,*" said James Field, speaking across the years. "*Sounds bad. But there's so much. Surely they couldn't wreck it all.*"

"Wait till you see what they've done to our forests."

I hoisted my backpack to my knees, then wrestled it around to get my arms through the straps. It seemed heavier, as though a couple of bars of desert gold had suddenly been added to my load. I scrambled up the ditchbank and plodded on, uphill, toward Captain Keeney Pass.

Heat waves rose before me. Water, a cool mirage, receded up the road as I chased it. Tar softened and bubbled and footprints told of my passing along the road's soft outer edge. The air was suddenly hot and thick and I pushed through it, each step requiring as much effort as walking through a pea field in June, the vines grabbing and clutching my legs. I groped around the back of my pack to where my last canteen dangled, half full, from its little metal clip. When I brought it to my lips I realized that the water had passed the warm stage and was now hot enough to make coffee. I guzzled it down. I might be out of water, I thought, but at least I no longer have five quarts to carry.

At last, I staggered through Captain Keeney Pass. Now I have it made, I thought. Just five miles to go, and all downhill.

My companions on this hike were smart enough to use animals and wagons to carry their belongings in 1845, but in 1852, John D. Henderson made this same hike and carried his own belongings. He may have been the first American backpacker through Captain Keeney Pass. His tombstone reads:

PIONEER GRAVE
OF
JOHN D. HENDERSON

DIED OF THIRST
AUGUST 9, 1852

UNAWARE OF NEARNESS OF THE MALHEUR RIVER

LEAVING INDEPENDENCE, MISSOURI IN MAY, 1852
MR. HENDERSON AND COMPANION, NAME UN-

KNOWN, HAD COMPLETED ONLY PART OF THE
JOURNEY WHEN THEIR TEAM DIED. THEY WERE
COMPELLED TO CONTINUE ON FOOT CARRYING
THEIR FEW POSSESSIONS. THE TWENTY MILES OF
DESERT SEPARATING THE SNAKE AND MALHEUR
RIVERS PROVED TOO GREAT A STRUGGLE FOR THE
WEARY TRAVELERS.

Henderson's grave is at the bottom of the hill, just under five miles from Captain Keeney Pass, about 100 yards east of the Malheur River. I visited his grave when I came to Vale the previous spring and thought it odd that a man could die of thirst just 100 yards from a river. But desert rivers are frequently hard to see, flowing along as they do in cracks in the earth often without so much as a line of willows or strip of green grass to announce their presence, hidden so well that you have to step into them to know where they. The Malheur was probably like that in Henderson's day.

Henderson barely crossed my mind that day. I strode downhill with new vigor, confident that I'd be in Vale for dinner. After all, I knew where the river was.

About a half mile down the road I stopped for a moment to rest beside a traffic sign. The slender shadow cast by its 4x4 post was the first shade I'd seen since early morning, when I crawled out of the little patch of willows in which I'd slept. It wasn't much, but it was shade, and I leaned against the post, afraid that if I put my pack down I'd be unable to pick it up again. My knees quivered. The heat waves were thicker now, and the road rippled ahead of me like a river of fire.

The elevation at Captain Keeney Pass is 2909 feet. Vale's elevation is 2242 feet. I was hiking downhill about 130 feet per mile. This should have been an easy walk. It wasn't.

I walked on another half mile or so and then stopped again to rest. The only shade was my own shadow, and there was no post to lean against, but my legs felt weak and my feet hurt, so I stopped and stood with my knees locked looking downhill. I hitched the backpack up a little higher on my back, tightened the waistband, and tried to focus my gaze in the distance where the road disappeared around a bend. A shadow swept over the little rolling hills and followed the road uphill toward me. A cloud. Thank God. Cloud, I thought, come to me, and for a couple of minutes the cloud floated between me and the searing sun. The temperature dropped 20 degrees and a little breeze licked the beads of sweat on my forehead, tugged at the moisture in my sopped t-shirt. Then it was gone and once again there was nothing between me and that blast furnace in the sky.

"Hey, Bud. Toss your gear in the back. I'll give you a lift into town."

I leaned on the pickup, grateful to have somewhere to lean, and looked through the passenger-side window into the happy blue eyes of a lanky young cowboy. There was a little slice of shade near the side of the pickup and I drew my body up close to take advantage of it. "Thanks," I heard myself say, "but I think I'll keep walking."

"Naawww," he said, like he couldn't quite believe what he was hearing. "C'mon. Get in." He pulled a half case of Blitz closer to him on the seat to make room for me. "This heat'll kill you."

"Thanks, but no thanks," I said, barely believing it myself.

"Well then, how about a cool one?" He reached into the box at his side and pulled out a bottle. Sweat beads glistened on the cool brown bottle. He thrust it toward me.

"That's very kind of you," I said, throttling an impulse to grab it and chug it, "but no, thanks."

Pure. The word played in my head like a commercial I couldn't erase. Purity. Pureness. Pure. This experience had to be pure. To accept a ride or a cold beer in the midst of this blazing heat would compromise its purity. "Gonna walk to Vale. Gotta keep it pure," I told him.

"*Fool.*" It was vague, fuzzy, coming to me as it did through the heat and across the years, but I'm sure I heard it. John Henderson, James Field, my grandfather and the others, united in their opinion, shook their heads in amazement.

"Well, if you gotta, you gotta," he said, returning the bottle to the box. He shook his head slowly. "You sure?" I nodded and pushed myself away from the pickup. "Good luck," he said with a shrug, and drove slowly away, dragging his little patch of shade with him.

I tottered on, downhill, treading as lightly as possible now, because each step was a hammer blow, ramming my toes to the front of my boots and driving my toenails backward, like hot spikes, into my toes. Gravity latched onto my pack, and in its grasp we lurched downhill, welded together, a bright blue bowling ball on two wobbly legs. Whoa, there. I stopped, afraid I'd pick up too much speed, wobble out of control and crash face first into the soft, hot tar. Heat blasted the thin soles of my old, worn hiking boots. The bottoms of my feet burned and baked and blistered. It hurt too much to stop, so on I went, sizzling across the desert like spit on a stove.

A cloud of vicious little flies floated out of the desert and attacked my unprotected legs. I slapped at them and the cloud thickened. They were undeterred by insect repellent from the little plastic bottle in my pocket. When I slapped at my right leg, they bit me on the left. When I swept them off my right arm, they bit me on the neck. When I slapped at my neck they drilled my right leg. With my hat, I discovered, I could discourage them, so I lurched on down the road, fanning the air with every step.

A mile. Two miles. Tired, gasping, I had to stop, so I dropped my backpack on the edge of the road and tumbled down the ditchbank. Across the ditch I tried to find shade under a sagebrush, but there wasn't enough to shelter even one leg from the raging sun, so I lay in the dirt and baked like a bug on a rock. Flies hovered. A couple of ants discovered my neck and then a few more followed, and soon a line of ants marched up and across my neck, down my t-shirt, over my shorts, straight down my left leg, and back onto the sand. They marched with singleminded determination, stopping only momentarily to investigate the little clumps of blood and fly body parts.

June 26, 1989
Why am I doing this? Why am I huddling in a tiny patch of shade, hiding from the noonday sun, my feet aching, little flies biting my legs, so far from home? I could be drinking lemonade, sitting in the shade, going to baseball games—
1. To have an adventure worth writing about
2. To challenge myself, to see if I can
3. To learn something of my 5x great grandfather
4. To know Oregon. Nearly everyone experiences Oregon through a windshield. To know it, really know it, you've got to taste it and touch it and feel its rocky crust beneath your feet, test yourself by stretching your legs across it.

High in the sky, just above where I thought Vale was, soared a heavy black cloud, pregnant with the promise of shade, or maybe, I dreamed, a drop or two of rain. As I watched, it floated gently my way. I lifted my head so I could see its shadow ripple over the sagebrush, following the road uphill to me. On it came, faster and faster and suddenly it blotted out the sun. I lay back, relaxed, enjoying the sudden coolness. The ants marched on, hardly noticing. Then, in an instant, the cloud soared on and its lovely, cool shadow slid over the hill, out of sight.

Seared once again by the blistering sun, I searched for another cloud. None was in sight, but, high in the clear blue sky, a turkey vulture circled, dragging his pinpoint shadow over the contours of the desert far below. I lay still, broiling on the sand, and watched. Adrift in the thermals, probably hoping for a roadkill, he'd stumbled onto what appeared to be a real meal. Soon he was joined by a friend, come to share the bounty. Then another made it a trio. Round and round they soared, high, aloof, feigning disinterest. They barely deigned to look down, but I watched them and I knew they were there for me.

I hope one day to provide lunch, and maybe dinner, for a host of desert creatures—coyotes, vultures, flies and their maggot offspring, even ants like the ones that had apparently grown unsure of their destination and were milling around on my leg just below my shorts—but not on this day. I stood and brushed off the ants, feeling momentarily dizzy. At the top of the ditchbank I struggled back into my backpack and staggered on down the road. Funny, I thought, it doesn't hurt any more.

The road dropped through a little gap, turned a few degrees right and leveled out. Buildings and trees in the distance told me I was almost to Vale. On the left, an Indian family of four worked with a couple of ponies in a little corral. A travel trailer and a new Ford pickup stood nearby. The family and the ponies stopped and watched as I trudged by. "That looks like a mighty heavy pack," the man said.

"It's a lot heavier now than it was this morning."

Sand Hollow Road joins Lytle Boulevard on the left, then joins the access road to John Henderson's grave. "Now I understand," I whispered, as I trudged on by his grave, "but I'm going to make it.

"*You probably will,*" Henderson agreed. "*You know where the river is.*"

At last, I crossed the bridge into Vale, stumbled across a

vacant lot toward the trees and grass of Vale's city park. Except for some Mexican children playing at the far end of the park, I had the place to myself. I took a deep breath of cool, shaded air, unbuckled my backpack and dropped it onto a picnic table. Then my knees buckled and I was flat on my back in the grass.

June 26, 1989, Vale, Oregon, 8 p.m.

An emergency measure, this motel room. Walking across Oregon's desert in the summer may be more of a test than I bargained for. When I finally got to Vale this afternoon I found a park near the bridge across the Malheur at the entrance to town. Grass & water. When I unbuckled my pack and set it down I nearly fainted. I sat for awhile on the grass and then went for water. When I came back I lay on the ground and could not keep my eyes open. I slept and woke and slept and woke for more than two hours before I regained enough strength to lift my pack and walk on into town where I found this motel. I still feel weak and slow and shaky. If I don't feel better tomorrow I'll lay over a day...

I understand now why Henderson died of thirst so near the river.

Miles today—16.5

June 27, 1989, Vale, Oregon, 8 a.m.

Repacked again. Removed more superfluous items, though I didn't think any remained. I'll hit the trail up the Malheur early tomorrow a little lighter. Thought again of buying a donkey, but with my limited knowledge of donkeys I'd probably be buying trouble. Better to get in shape, walk farther, carry less.

Woke up this morning still shaky from yesterday. Achy, too. I wonder just how close I came to passing out on the road. Would I have made it if the road was a mile longer? Three miles? Along tomorrow's route there is shade and water.

Walking along there yesterday, I tried to imagine Sam

Parker and the rest toiling to get their wagons over that pass. It wasn't easy with cars and trucks whizzing by and four-engine airplanes circling over me.

Yesterday when I would stop for a moment on the road the bottoms of my feet would burn. The tar on the road melted and came up in little bubbles. My shoes were worn out, thin-soled and worn so my little toes on both feet were jammed together. Feet hurt and I wasn't looking forward to putting those shoes on again. So in a saddle shop here I found some Wolverine boots on sale and bought them. I know that these are not the best conditions for breaking in a new pair of boots, but they couldn't be any worse on my feet than my old ones, which are too well broken in.

The main buckle on my pack is broken. I called Chris to ask her to mail me a replacement to pick up in Burns. Never thought I'd find a replacement in Vale, but the saddle shop here had the exact one.

My new boots are warming in the sun, soaking up oil. I'm still a little quivery from yesterday, but feeling a little stronger every hour.

I'll be seven pounds lighter when I hit the road tomorrow.

Cooler today than yesterday. A little cloudy now. Every time the shadow of a cloud came up that hill yesterday I prayed for it to stick with me, but none did.

As it was for my companions in 1845, Vale was for me a place of recuperation. When I awoke in my motel bed about 11 that morning my whole body ached. When I stood I was dizzy. I went back to sleep. About 1 p.m. I wandered down the street to the restaurant. After a couple of buffaloeburgers ("less cholesterol than beef") and two giant chocolate milkshakes, I felt better. I went back to my motel room and back to sleep. Late in the afternoon, feeling stronger, I ventured forth again:

June 27, 1989 (continued)

Took a turn around town in my new boots. They hurt like hell, so I put them back in the box with a note. I'll leave them at the bootshop door when I leave in the early morning. The variety store across the street sells basketball shoes. I found some that don't hurt my feet, so I'll be out of here tomorrow wearing my new white Puma basketball shoes.

My route tomorrow is due west over a straight road across East Bench and West Bench—cross Bully Creek at six miles and then down into Malheur Canyon.

Hungry, I walked again to the restaurant. After large steak (beef, not buffalo) and two more milkshakes I was pretty sure I'd live till breakfast.

> The trail described by Meek led west up the Malheur River, over low, intervening hills, crossed the Blue Mountains to the valley of the Jay's River (Crooked River). That would take about a week. From this valley they would follow up a branch to one near the south fork of Day's River, then would cross over Jay's River and go down it to Fall River. By traveling the high country between Day's and Fall Rivers north, they would cross the latter stream and go on into the Dalles on the Columbia.[4]

It probably never occurred to Meek that he could not pull it off:

> By a vote it was decided to follow Mr. Meek. A contract was signed to pay him for his services, and he agreed to pilot the company safely through in thirty days, or, as was written in his own words, give his head for a football. All were to take turns hauling his goods. He and his wife were on horseback.[5]

Meek left the hot springs at Vale on August 24, 1845, leading the first group of wagons into the desert. Sam Parker left later the same day, traveling in a group of 53 wagons led by Captain Nicholas Ownby. James Field followed on August 25, traveling in a group of 52 wagons led by James B. Riggs. On August 26, William Helm and his family left the hot springs in a group of 58 wagons led by Captain Solomon Tetherow. One other group of 51 wagons left on August 25 or 26. I believe Jesse Harritt traveled with the last group.

Taken together, the snapshot journal entries of Parker, Field, and Harritt represent a panoramic view of each day's travel, from three perspectives separated by approximately one day's journey, vastly different temperaments, and different levels of writing skill. As Parker was first on the trail, Field second, and Harritt last, that is the order in which their views will be presented here. *Ghosts speak like this, in italics. Everybody knows that.* Entries from my journal will appear as regular text, like this, but will be signaled by the date in which they appeared in the journal.

August 24, 1845

tuck what is caled the meeks Cut of misses Butts tuck Sick this day A Bad Cut of fore all that tuck it

Samuel Parker

Graham Boulevard is another country road with a city name, running due west, straight as a bullet over low hills now fenced, planted, irrigated, green with new crops in June. The Meek Cutoff meandered a little north here, a little south there, but west was where they were going and today's traveler over their trail is confined between the fences and irrigation ditches to Graham Boulevard. I tramped out of Vale in the early morning, wearing my new Puma basketball shoes.

114

August 25, 1845
"Here we left the former route; bearing a little south of west we
steered our course over a tolerable good road 13 miles and encamped
on the same stream; found grass and a few willows."
Jesse Harritt

June 28, 1989, Vale, 5:45 a.m.
Just light. No clouds. I am recuperated. I was worried
that I'd done something serious to myself, that my body would
not rebound, but it has and I feel at full strength and ready to
go. My experience coming up East Cow Hollow taught me a
few things. For one, the sun means business around here. I
won't challenge it again in quite the same way. Also, I have a
better idea of my own limits than I did a few days ago. I'm 47
years old and I taught school all year. I need a few days to
acclimatize my body to the switch from classroom to desert.
Bully Creek Valley, 9:05 a.m.
Seven miles before breakfast. Sitting in the shade beside
an irrigation ditch. Swallows darting about, killdeer "twee-
twee" across the road, magpies flying away and redwinged
blackbirds diving from the power lines. Everywhere the sound
of irrigation. The road so far is lined with houses surrounded
by shade trees—eucalyptus, cottonwood trimmed to look like
date palms, locust, birch. Why, with all this land, are the houses
so close to the road?
A motor home goes by, towing a boat. How differently
we travel.
11:05 a.m.
I burrowed in beneath a tumbledown old willow tree
for a break and fell asleep. Clouds in the west and a cool breeze,
a great day for a long walk. I am walking along the Vale Oregon
Canal. To the north the country is probably about as the 1845
folks saw it, "wormwood barrens"—sagebrush as far as any-

one can see. South of the canal is all under cultivation or irrigated pasture with cattle and horses grazing. I smell smoke.

About seven miles west of Vale, Graham Boulevard meets the Vale-Oregon Canal, which parallels the Malheur River, snaking along the bluffs about 300 feet above the river. When I stepped off Graham Boulevard to follow the Canal access road, 30 miles from the Idaho border, I hiked for the first time off the pavement. Now the agricultural green of the Malheur Valley was behind me and I hiked once again through a brown, shadeless land, along a dirt road built atop the south bank of the canal. I joined the canal about two miles north of the river. Three miles later the canal and the river converged. Less than a quarter of a mile separate them as they flow through Malheur Canyon.

June 28, 1989 (continued) 12:53 p.m.

On a promontory overlooking a diversion dam on the Malheur just before Malheur Canyon. A dozen huge birds soar downstream toward me and then catch an updraft and ride it in lazy circles. Now they're above a hill across the river, circling down, down, down, skim the water and up again, searching for the perfect spot. Swans, maybe, white swans with wings fringed in black. They look more like pelicans, but pelicans in the desert? Now in a lovely little clutch they drift downstream.

August 25, 1845
"went over hills all day and Came to the malhuren at nite"
Samuel Parker

The railroad and the river flow together through Malheur Canyon today. From my perch high up the canyon rim, I see the railroad cross the river twice, cut across a meander, leaving the river where it turned northwestward and rejoining it as it

116

turned again southwestward, eliminating about a mile of riverbank. Then the railroad and the river disappeared side by side into the ever-narrowing canyon. Indeed, those wagons were able to go anywhere if they had to follow this river through that canyon. Boulders abound, the canyon narrows and then narrows some more. Unless traveling the railroad right-of-way, the canyon is impassable even by Jeep.

August 26, 1845
Verry Rockey and hilly Camped on A small Streame
Samuel Parker

Went about ten miles, still keeping up Malheur, crossing and re-crossing it twice, and camping upon it. We were obliged to take to the bluffs to get across several narrow bends of the river, and there we found some as hard road as any we had yet traveled. Indeed, I begin to think wagons can go anywhere.
James Field

I can see where you took to the bluffs, James. Probably you pulled out of the canyon at about the same place I did earlier this year when I drove my Jeep along the river. The climb was tough enough for the Jeep, powered by a hundred or so horses, 4-wheel drive and an assortment of gears low enough to power it up a wall. That you could urge your oxen up that grade borders on miraculous.

The trail here turns southwest, paralleling the Malheur River through the canyon, still following approximately the same high route as the Vale Oregon Canal. By now it's hot again, the red line on my little thermometer creeping into the 90s. Rocks radiate heat and the access road along the canal wavers in the distance through the heat waves. Water in the canal is dark green, almost brown. Heat and agricultural waste transform it into a gelid goo that rolls rather than flows along in the canal, a substance almost thick enough to walk on. I take the first swig from my last canteen—city water from Vale—shrug into my backpack, and walk on.

Ouch. Somehow, while I sat pondering pelicans and wagon trains along the Malheur, a handful of little rocks got into my new basketball shoes. I set my backpack down, climbed back to my perch on the rock, and took off my shoes. What felt like little rocks were bits of shredded rubber. In 15 or so miles I'd walked clear through the insole of my new shoes. I pulled them back on, laced them up, and hiked gingerly on.

A mile or so down the road I followed the canal around a corner and a new red Ford pickup glided up and stopped beside me. The driver, a tall, heavy man, sprawled across the seat, his left arm draped out the window and his head resting as on a pillow in the driver's side corner of the cab. His right arm lay across the steering wheel, elbow and wrist limp as dishrags.

"Hi," he said, with a friendly, lazy smile.

I leaned on the passenger side door, glad once again for a pickup to lean on. He wore pressed blue jeans and a clean white snapbutton shirt, clothes a rancher would wear to negotiate at the bank. A tan Stetson lay beside him on the pickup seat. He slowly turned his head head to look at me, like a man dragging himself up from a dream. I had the impression that he'd been driving along the canal road half asleep and wasn't yet sure if I was real or just part of the dream he'd been having when I appeared. In any case, he seemed reluctant to wake up.

"What in the world are you doing out here?" he asked quietly.

"Hiking an old wagon train route," I told him wearily. My feet hurt, and stopping intensified the pain. By now the foamy insole was worn to dust in each basketball shoe, and hard little ridges molded like ribs on the inside of each sole cut into my foot with every step.

We stopped in the blazing sun and talked for a while of wagon trains and cattle and ranching and writing. He had the languid, easy manner of a man whose deadlines, if he had any, were dictated by a clock of his own or perhaps by the sun, a refreshing country manner. In contrast, I was driven by my acquired city manner, driven to make 20, 22, 24 miles each day, to keep on schedule, cover that ground, finish the hike in time (In time for what?), keep walking. It was summer, but school bells still rang in my head and I soon felt that I should be plodding on.

But a battered copy of <u>Walden</u> rode in my backpack. I'd spent part of my recuperation day in Vale reading again Thoreau's spiritual odyssey, and, so, another ghost had joined us along the Terrible Trail. *"Why should we knock under and go with the stream?"* Thoreau asked in 1845.

"Why, indeed?" I wondered. I walked around to the driver side of the pickup and to say goodbye.

"Watch your step," the rancher said, looking curiously at my basketball shoes. "You'll be in rattlesnake country soon."

Probably it is more accurate to say that Thoreau'd been with us all along. He's been with me for years, ever since my high school English teacher pressed a copy of <u>Walden</u> into my hands in Pendleton so many years ago and I, protesting all the while that I couldn't understand this stuff, was jolted into seeing more clearly the world in which I lived. "Not me," I thought, smugly, with the arrogance of youth, when Thoreau pointed out to me the ratrace that consumed most of my elders, but the road of life is long and I couldn't see around all the bends. Now Thoreau, having been silenced so frequently over the years, huddles meekly in the corner of my mind on most days, and I obediently commute to work. Occasionally, though, he stands up and roars, refuses to be silenced. This was one of those times.

On the Fourth of July, 1845, when the folks in this wagon

train were about to leave the Great Plains behind them, Thoreau turned his back on the Independence Day celebration in Concord, Massachusetts, and moved to a cabin that he had built with his own hands on the shore of Walden Pond, a mile or so south of the village. *"I went to the woods,"* he tells us, *"because I wished to live deliberately, to front only the essential facts of life, and see if I could not learn what it had to teach, and not, when I came to die, discover that I had not lived."*

But, Henry, I tell him, you could have been on the wagon train. If you wished to "live deep and suck out all the marrow of life, to live so sturdily and Spartanlike as to put to rout all that was not life, to cut a broad swath and shave close, to drive life into a corner, and reduce it to its lowest terms..." where could you have done it more deliberately than on the Oregon Trail?

"Still we live meanly like ants..." he tells me, and I see as though from an airplane, the antlike queues of wagons and oxen plodding across the continent. *"I see young men, my townsmen, whose misfortune it is to have inherited farms, houses, barns, cattle, and farming tools; for these are more easily acquired than got rid of...They have got to live a man's life, pushing all these things before them, and get on as well as they can. How many a poor immortal soul have I met well-nigh crushed and smothered under its load, creeping down the road of life, pushing before it a barn seventy-five feet by forty, its Augean stables never cleansed, and one hundred acres of land, tillage, mowing, pasture, and woodlot."*

Okay, okay. So establishing a homestead in Oregon wasn't something you wanted to do, however rich the soil or thick the timber. You could have raised cattle.

"I am wont to think that men are not so much the keepers of herds as herds are the keepers of men, the former are so much freer. Men and oxen exchange work; but if we consider necessary work only, the oxen will be seen to have greatly the advantage, their farm is so much the larger."

I see.

"Actually, the laboring man has not leisure for a true integrity day by day...He has no time to be anything but a machine."

Hmm. Being a laboring man myself, I can attest to the truth of that. You needed—we all need—time for reflection and observation. But what about the adventure, Henry? This was the main event of your lifetime, and you could have been there. Instead, you holed up in a cabin so close to your mother's house that you could walk over and have dinner in her kitchen.

"It is not worth the while to go round the world to count the cats in Zanzibar...If you would learn to speak all tongues and conform to the customs of all nations, if you would travel farther than all travellers, be naturalized in all climes...obey the precept of the old philosopher, and Explore thyself. Herein are demanded the eye and the nerve. Only the defeated and deserters go to the wars, cowards that run away and enlist..."

Yes, I know. Yours was a spiritual odyssey, the examined life. But what about these men and women who uprooted their families in the east and struck out on the Oregon Trail? They were dreamers, not cowards. How do you feel about them?

"...if one advances confidently in the direction of his dreams, and endeavors to live the life which he has imagined, he will meet with a success unexpected in common hours. He will put some things behind, will pass an invisible boundary; new, universal, and more liberal laws will begin to establish themselves around and within him; or the old laws will be expanded and intepreted in his favor in a more liberal sense, and he will live with the license of a higher order of beings... If you have built castles in the air, your work need not be lost; that is where they should be. Now put the foundations under them."

That sounds like approval, with maybe even an under-tone of admiration, but my feet burned now as though someone had poured liquid fire in my basketball shoes and I was having trouble concentrating. In the distance, traffic glinted like sunlit insects on Highway 20. Wait. Henry—before you go—one more thing: What about now? What do you think of what we've become?

Bad Road   Went 12

Okay, okay, Sam. We'll get back to the road in a minute. Henry spun on his heel and, with upraised index finger and open mouth, strode back across my mind. He looked angry and he certainly had something to say, but the pain in my feet drew him back into the shadows. *"You haven't heard the last from me,"* he promised as he faded from my consciousness.

"Went about 18 miles today. The road, although leading across the bluffs which in a country where mountains are a rarity would pass for pretty good sized ones, was tolerably fair, but there is an abundance of small, sharp stones in it, black and hard as iron, and very wearing to the feet of the cattle. We camped upon Carter's fork, from its appearance a branch of Burnt river."

James Field

The little black stones are still there, and I sympathized with the cattle. I sat on a little bridge and pulled off my shoes. The pain had subsided in the last couple of miles and each step felt soft, squishy, damp. I thought my feet were sweating, because I knew I'd not stepped into anything wet, and I welcomed the easing off of the pain, but I was shocked when I found my socks soaked in blood. The insole was trod to dust now, and the little ridges on the inside of my shoes had worn away the skin on the bottoms of my feet. Disgusted, I flipped the basketball shoes over my shoulder into the canal, where they landed with a splat and refused to sink. They rode silently out of sight, little white boats adrift on a furrow of glop. I doubted that a rock would sink in that canal.

I peeled off my socks and swabbed my feet with disinfectant from the little first aid kit in my pack. The damage wasn't as extensive as I'd feared, but it was sufficient to make hiking a very uncomfortable enterprise. I waited until the bleeding stopped and then pulled on a clean pair of socks and the river sandals I'd brought along to wear in camp.

Highway 20 was about a mile south of where I sat. The wagon train route continues south, toward highway 20 along the canal access road, for about 3/4 of a mile, then turns due west, diverging from Highway 20 for about five miles. The trail then turns northwest, along the road to Harper. Highway 20 turns southwest and then west toward Burns. The trail doesn't approach the highway again for nearly 100 miles.

I drained the last swallow of Vale water from my last canteen, slipped the pack straps back over my shoulders, and stood up. No pain. Then I tottered on down the canal road, careful to avoid putting pressure on the sorest parts of my feet. Fences criss-cross the land here, and several small corrals line the canal road. There are trees, dusty-leaved, baked and beaten-looking in the heat of a June afternoon, shading a couple of small buildings, too far from the canal road to benefit a hiker. Within half a mile my feet burned and the bleeding started again. Thirsty again, I decided to have a drink and consider my options.

Canal water. I wondered if it was even wet. It slides along in the canal, so thick and dark and quiet. Full of nutrients, like thick soup. A man could get his daily minimum requirement of protein from one swallow of that stuff. I wondered how many water purification tablets to put into my canteen. Directions on the bottle said one tablet per canteen, but the people who made the pills never saw water like this. I dropped my pack at the far side of the road and took the canteen to the edge of the canal.

"You must be mighty thirsty."

He motored up astride a little red four-wheel Honda with a .22 rifle slung in a scabbard across its handle bars and stopped in the middle of the road to see what I was up to. A small man in a greasy red "Unoco" hat and coveralls, he perched, birdlike, on the fat-tired little machine while we talked. "You see any rattlesnakes up there?" he made a quick little gesture up the road behind me.

"No," I told him, "no rattlesnakes." Not that there was no evidence of their presence. I told him about the snakeskins I'd noticed, sloughed off like old clothes and left on the ground or hung like wash across the lower branches of sagebrush.

"You can kill one every time you go up that road," he said, with a quick little shake of his head.

Not me, I thought. I'd rather kill a man than a rattlesnake.

"I'm surprised you didn't see any." He glanced at the sun, which, it seemed to me, hadn't dropped even an inch toward the horizon in the last couple of hours. "Maybe it's a little early."

I was walking through prime rattlesnake habitat wearing a pair of sandals. I was thirsty, tired, hot, and my feet burned and bled. I could hitch-hike to Burns and come back, continue my trip along the Terrible Trail by Jeep. Roads followed the entire route, anyway. If I hiked the trail northwest now, I wouldn't see Highway 20 again for about five days, nearly 100 miles. That it might be prudent to abandon the hike glimmered in my mind.

"Climb on behind me here and we'll get you a drink of good water." He scooted forward on the little machine and I saw where I could just squeeze my butt in behind his.

I looked at the thick canal water oozing silently by and then at the birdlike man smiling at me from the motorcycle and knew that the gods or Coyote or somebody up there was on my side.

I dug another empty canteen out of my pack, threw one leg over the seat and slid in behind him. We were wedged tight, belly-to-back, on the little machine, and when we lurched down the road I wrapped my right arm around him to keep from falling. "You can call me Lester," he shouted over his shoulder. He smelled like leather and oil and horses and as we bounced along he talked over his shoulder, telling me how he got his farm (inherited part, bought part, traded for another part), how he made it pay (He was a model of diversification—part farming, part cattle, part hauling hay and other crops for other farmers.), and how tough economic times were forcing some of the bigger outfits in the valley into bankruptcy. Suddenly, the little machine swerved to the right, hopped down the canal bank, through a gap in the fence, and pulled up behind a shed made of weatherbeaten one-by-six planks. "Best water in the valley," he told me as he pulled open the door and handed me the end of an old green hose that lay coiled on the floor of the little building. He spun a handle and cold, clear water spewed from the hose.

"God. That's delicious." I drank until my belly swelled, but I couldn't get enough so I drank some more. Then I filled the canteens and drank a little more. Clear, sweet water continued to pour from the hose, into the gravel in front of the shed and I was aware as never before of the cavalier attitude I'd always taken toward this lovely, most precious fluid. Lester, apparently, was unconcerned, but I couldn't stand to see it wasted, so I ran into the building and spun the tap closed. I was so full of water I sloshed as I walked, but still I wanted more.

"Where'd you say you were goin'?" Lester asked, looking dubiously at my sandals.

"Well, at one time I was thinking about hiking all the way to The Dalles, but just since you brought me down here I've been thinking maybe I'd just go over to the highway and hitchhike into Burns to pick up my Jeep."

"Good idea," he said, curtly. "I don't see how you could hike much in those shoes."

The next bridge was three miles or so downriver, in Harper, but, if it was up to him, he said, he'd just hike down there and ford the river. He pointed south, downhill, where the river and the road ran side-by-side. We climbed back onto the little Honda and buzzed back down the canal road to where I'd left my backpack.

As I walked along, I noticed that the sagebrush ranged from almost gray to a vibrant emerald color, and that the stems were sometimes brittle and black and sometimes soft, velvety green. It was all sagebrush to me, but I asked Lester about the different kinds.

"Rabbitbrush, buckbrush, greasewood, and sagebrush," he answered over his shoulder, pointing to little patches of each as we bounced down the road. "You can make charcoal good enough to cook over from greasewood. And if one of your animals comes up with foot rot, you can make a fine liniment by mixing up some of that charcoal with some greasewood and sagebrush—no buckbrush—and cooking it in a little water. Let it stand for a day or two and it's the best stuff you ever saw for treating foot rot."

By the time we arrived at my backpack, the decision was made. I would hitchhike to Burns and get my Jeep.

"You can get across down there," Lester told me. Traffic

sparkled in the sunlight across the river. "Get yourself a big stick so you can feel out the bottom. It'll be about waist deep, and it's pretty fast right along there, so be careful. And watch out for rattlesnakes."

I thanked him profusely for the water, the ride, the conversation, and then pulled on my backpack and struck out, away from the canal, toward the river. He turned the little red Honda and sped toward the pumphouse. Suddenly, he wheeled around and bounced down off the ditchbank road along a track through the sagebrush toward me.

"Can't let you walk through there in those shoes," he said. "There are rattlesnakes everywhere this time of year. Throw your pack on the back and c'mon aboard." A wide chrome luggage rack bolted to the back of the Honda held a shovel and an ax. I lay my pack on the rack and climbed on behind Lester. We bounced over rocks and ruts and furrows cut by rainwater in the desert slope toward the river. Down we shot, through little gullies, around large clumps of sagebrush, a half mile or so downhill and then back up, over the railroad tracks and down to a gate in the barbwire fence near the river. "End of the line," Lester announced. The Honda clattered to a stop across the round rocks of a seasonal riverbottom, dry now in the summer heat. In front of us lay a line of willows and grass, brush along the riverbank; then the Malheur River, and the bank, steep on the other side, right up to the highway. Lester and I shook hands. He warned me again about rattlesnakes, reminded me to find a big stick to help me cross the river, and then he was gone, towing a little roostertail of dust through the sagebrush, buckbrush, rabbitbrush and greasewood, uphill toward the canal.

The river was thirty or forty feet wide, swift and deep and the water was the same thick, brown stuff that slid along the canal. I paced carefully along the bank, wary of possible rattlesnake resting spots, until I found a place where it looked possible to cross. A selection of sturdy river-probing sticks lay along the bank, stranded by low water. With waistband and chest straps unbuckled so I could shrug out of my pack in a hurry if I fell, I took a few tentative steps into the water. The bank sloped steeply toward the middle of the river and then flattened, chest deep. I poked and prodded the riverbottom, feeling before stepping, trying to find stability between the big round rocks that lay along the riverbottom. Another step and the water was around my armpits, rushing by, pulling me, pulling my pack. I backed out.

Upstream fifty feet or so the current was a little swifter but not nearly so deep, judging from the way it riffled around a little bend. The riverbank on the other side was straight up— riprap, scree and sand all the way to the guardrail that kept wayward cars from hurtling into the river. The water rose to my knees, to my crotch, to my belly button. I prodded the bottom ahead, then stepped, again and again, working my way across. A handhold, then a foothold appeared in a riprap boulder at the bottom of the riverbank. I grabbed, climbed, pulled myself over the boulder. Then the scree, the loose, slippery, dusty scree—on hands and knees, I scrambled up-ward, through the dust and sand. At the top, seeking that last firm handhold, I clawed and grasped—what's this? This crusty, tubular, dry as dust, light as a feather thing? A piece of rope dropped from a passing horse trailer? Dry leaves? A roadkilled rattlesnake, rattles gone, eyesockets empty, ribs breaking through along the spine like a long, delicate comb, where magpies and vultures and sun and wind have eaten away the scales and meat. I sailed it back, over my head, heard it clash drily on the riprap below, then stood, dirty and wet, at the side of Highway 20, about 90 miles east of Burns.

Across the United States, Europe and East Africa—for years, I hitchhiked. It had been a few years, but it was a practiced thumb I stuck into the sporadic traffic flow along

Highway 20 that summer evening. I knew, for instance, that drivers are more apt to stop in the morning than in the evening, when the weather's cool than when it's hot, that a man traveling alone has a tough time catching a lift any time, and that the very best hitchhiking situation for a young man is to partner up with a pretty girl. Ninety-four degrees, the sun about to set. Not only did I not have a pretty girl for a partner, I wasn't even young any more. I kept thumbing until sunset and then, in the twilight, I walked off into the desert and rolled out my sleeping bag.

Once again I was out of water. Upstream, kicking myself for not filling more canteens at Lester's well, I found a way down to the river to replenish my supply.

June 29, 1989
Water in Malheur looks like horse piss even when poured (in a thin stream) from a cup.

But I drank, ate, and lay back to watch the stars. A soft, sibilant, sage-scented wind drove away the heat. Over on the highway an 18-wheeler steamed out of the east, wreathed in lights and noise, a ship of the night sailing the Oregon desert. Somewhere Old Man Coyote laughed, no doubt at a joke of his own making.

It was daylight when I woke and found the rattlesnake skin draped across my cheek and arm. I lay still and pryed open my other eye. Empty rattlesnake eye holes peered vacantly into my face. Had the rattlesnake slithered by in the night and, attracted by my warmth, curled up and shed his old clothes in my bed? Probably it had been there the night before, hung like so many others in the branches of the sagebrush or greasewood. The wind could have brought it to me. Or maybe this is the joke I heard Old Man Coyote laughing about as I drifted off to sleep. I brewed some coffee, then packed and went to the road.

"Praise the Lord, Brother!"

Praise the Lord, indeed. I'd just hailed a taxi. "Globe Taxi, San Mateo, California. 792-6364," read the little metal sign bolted to the top of the yellow Ford sedan. There was a little fish next to the telephone number.

The driver climbed out and popped open the trunk. "Toss your gear in there and climb in."

"I wasn't expecting a taxi."

"You got the fare?" he asked, grinning.

"Well, uh, no," I answered, uncertain if he was joking.

"We'll waive it, then. I'm lonesome. Need someone to talk to."

Soon we were zipping towards Burns at 65 miles an hour—three days' hike each hour. "What's a California taxi doing in the Oregon desert?"

"A couple of days ago I went to pick up an old lady who rides with me occasionally and she asked me to take her to Virginia City, Montana. Longest fare I ever had. I'm on my way back home now." He barely fit behind the wheel of the little car. He was clean-shaven, his hair jet black and neatly combed, held in place by oil or hair tonic that made it glisten like it was damp. He wore a white snap-button shirt, riding pants and alligator-skin boots. A braided leather bolo tie with silver ends and a tie clasp of silver-mounted turquoise lay in a loose cinch around his neck. A little silver cross dangled from a chain around the rear-view mirror and the car smelled of cologne or after-shave lotion. "Name's Bill," he said, extending a large, soft hand. "How far you goin'?"

"To Burns. To my Jeep."

We talked. I leaned back, relaxed, enjoying the flow of desert past the windshield. Horizons hours away on foot were behind us in minutes. A middle-aged English teacher standing among the beer cans, disposable diapers, dead rattlesnakes and other roadside debris on a bank of the Malheur River early on a summer morning, we decided, was probably no less improbable than a California taxi stopping to pick him up. On the radio, news of a confrontation at an abortion clinic and the arrest of some anti-abortion activists: "Abortion," Bill snorted. "It's just plain wrong."

In Juntura we stopped for coffee and pie. The waiter wore a wide belt of rattlesnakeskin. Snakeskin cases attached to the belt held his glasses and a Swiss Army knife.

"How ya doin?" A gaunt cowboy straddled the barstool next to mine. Hunched over the counter, protectively encircling a slice of lemon meringue pie and a cup of coffee with long, thin arms, he appraised me with a sidelong glance. His fork, wrapped in a big, calloused fist, stopped mid-plunge, poised like a diver above the pie. He looked angry. "Gotta go to town today," he confided. "That's worse'n workin'".

Bill was a Christian. "Used to hell around and drink and sing in the bars, but the Lord changed all that. Sang with Johnny Cash and June Carter once, down in California, but now I'm living the good life." He reached for his wallet. "Got any pictures of your family?" he asked, pulling out a stack of photographs. "These are my kids," he said proudly.

"All these are yours?" A whole village of children and women smiled at me from the photographs.

"Yep." He smiled proudly and showed me which children belonged to which mother. "Four wives," he said with a grin. "Twenty-one kids."

We drove on, over great rolling desert hills. The chalky white landscape of the Snake and Malheur country became volcanic red-brown as we sped west. Heat waves rippled the road. Mesmerized, I fell asleep and then awoke as the car slowed to enter Burns. The Jeep stood as I'd left it, beneath a large willow tree, protected from the fierce mid-day heat. I dragged my pack out of the trunk and leaned it against the back

131

bumper.

"God bless you, Mike," Bill said as we shook hands. I wished him luck. He glanced at the sky as if to say, "Who needs luck when you have God?"

"Take things in stride." he said, "The Lord'll help you along." Then, in a little cloud of dust, he was gone.

Alone, I touched the Jeep, tentatively at first, as though I was afraid it would vanish like a mirage. Then I sat on the fender for a moment. I don't usually like cars very much, but I was very happy to see this one. Inside, I found five gallons of sweet, clear McKenzie River water from Eugene; field guides to birds, insects, wildflowers and mammals; binoculars; my little aluminum and plastic camp chair; a fishing rod; a plastic box of hooks and weights; wedges of cheese wrapped in foil; cans of chili, kippers, and fruit; three or four boxes of crackers; Zip-Loc bags full of peanuts, granola, and dried fruit. I filled five canteens with well water, pushed my backpack through the door and climbed in.

In the space of a couple of hours I picked up the extra equipment I mailed to myself from Vale, drove 70 or so miles east along Highway 20, crossed the Malheur at Harper Junction, and rejoined the Terrible Trail along the Vale Oregon Canal east of Harper.

I spent an hour or so searching for some graves marked on the map near the canal north of Harper, in the hope that they might provide a connection to the wagon train, but found only cattle and grassless, barren land. A couple of miles northwest of Harper the canal road joins the paved Harper-Westfall Road and runs northwest along Willow Spring Creek between great white hills, covered in June with yellow grass, bright green rabbit brush and gray green sagebrush.

August 28, 1845

Bad Road went 7

Samuel Parker

Went about six miles, camping upon the same branch as before. The sharp stones spoken of yesterday were more plentiful today and a few more such days' travel as this will entirely use up our cattles' feet.

James Field

Having had my own feet pretty well used up, I sympathized with the cattle and was very appreciative of my Jeep that day. I ripped along at 70 miles an hour, doors off, furnace-breath wind whipping through my hair, imagining Parker and Field and Harritt plodding through this white, powdery land at 12 or 18 miles each day. Great white colonnades, carved by wind and rain, stood like sentinels along the road. First visible miles off, a day's travel for the wagon train, I reached them in minutes.

Just west of Westfall, near where Indian and Cottonwood Creeks flow into Bully Creek, the trail turns almost due west. Roads, fences, and private property make it difficult to follow the exact route:

June 29, 1989

Now across a high plain, wending generally westward. Greasewood and sagebrush. Castle Rock glimpsed occasionally in the distance drawing ever nearer. Hill after hill after hill. More vast wormwood barrens. Temperature 95 degrees, windy. Bench marker: elevation 4060.17 ft.

August 29, 1845

Verry bad Road Broak 3 wagens this day 5
Samuel Parker

Went about 12 miles today, over mountains to which those we

133

had previously crossed were small hills, camping near a little spring in the mountains which affords sufficient water for the use of camp, but our cattle would have been obliged to do without any had it not been for a storm of rain which came on in the evening, the first storm for months. The mountains are covered with small, black, hard nine-cornered stones, about the size of those used to macadamize a road, and our cattle cringe at every step.
James Field

Traveled 12 miles over the mountain; had bad road; encamped at a good spring affording plenty water for camp use; none for stock; found tolerable good grass and a few willows.
Jesse Harritt

At sunset, ponderous, bloated clouds appeared in the west and I set up my tent so I could sleep well and dry. The clouds went away in the twilight and I dragged my sleeping bag out beneath the sky in a clump of huge juniper trees where I lay and watched satellites and shooting stars blink and streak through the heavens with a clarity so stark it was almost audible. Parker, Harritt, Field and Helm might have sheltered beneath these same juniper trees in 1845. With that thought, on the soft, cool desert wind, I drifted off to sleep.

The trail now crosses the Bendire Range, southeast of Castle Rock, and descends the west slope of Immigrant Hill to Warm Springs Creek. In 1960, when Keith Clark and Lowell Tiller followed the Meek Cutoff for their book, <u>Terrible Trail: The Meek Cutoff, 1845</u>, scars left by wagons descending with their wheels locked were visible on the slope of Immigrant Hill. I could not find the scars when I was there in April and June, 1989.

August 30, 1845

Rock all day pore grass more swaring then you ever heard 11
Samuel Parker

Went about 12 miles today, over mountains as high as any yet met with, but some of them were grassy without rocks, whilst others were were covered with the big round stones so nice to jounce a wagon over, spoken of back towards Fort Hall. We camped upon a small branch and found grass and water both plenty and good, which was what our cattle stood in much need of, as for several days we have had hard roads and bad camps, which has cut down stock lower than at any time. Three or four oxen have laid down in the road and given out every day for the past few days.
James Field

Had a fine shower of rain last night. This morning the fog was so thick that we had great difficulty in collecting our cattle; made a start at nine o'clock; traveled ten miles over huge mountains and encamped on Hill Fork, a beautiful little branch; found good grass and willows; a few rods from us was a warm spring bursting from the side of a lofty mountain—a little above blood heat.
Jesse Harritt

Early the next morning I followed Bully Creek west, crossed Big Flat north of Bendire Ridge and Bendire Mountain, and dropped into a couple of the fairest valleys in Oregon, Agency Valley and the Valley of the North Fork of the Malheur River. Seen from the north, from the slopes of Hunter Mountain, Beulah Reservoir, at the bottom of Agency Valley, sparkles in the distance like a deep blue jewel.

In the spring I followed nearly the same route. Just after crossing Bendire Creek, my Jeep refused to run. I walked to the nearest ranchhouse, eight miles away, where I met Bob Browning, his wife and two children. From their house, I telephoned

Juntura to try to convince a mechanic to come to my rescue.

"My truck's broke down and my wife'll kill me if I bring my Lincoln up there," he told me. "If you can get your Jeep to Juntura, I can probably fix it." Twenty-nine miles of bad road and a couple of stream crossings separated my Jeep from the garage.

"If you can wait till I finish a couple of little jobs I've got to do around here," Bob said, "I'll take you back up there and we'll see if we can't get it to run."

As we rattled up the road I asked him about the recently cut juniper trees that lay scattered across the valley. "I know that looks like a waste of good trees to you, "he said, "but they're weeds to me. My business is growing grass for my cows to eat, and those junipers have shallow roots that spread out around the tree and steal every bit of moisture from the grass. You look around those trees. Grass can't grow up close to a juniper. We don't get enough water up here to waste any, so every year I cut down about 50 acres of juniper trees. At that rate," he chuckled, "every twenty years I'll clearcut a thousand acres."

"The way I figure it," he said, "Nobody's found a way to get off this planet, so we have to live here. As long as that's true, we'll have to use what's here."

The Jeep would not start, so he dragged a long chain out of the bed of the pickup. I wrapped one end of the chain around the Jeep bumper. He hooked other to the trailer hitch on his pickup. "Guess I just better tow you on down to Juntura."

"That's 29 miles," I reminded him. "You sure you want to do that?"

"My only other choice is to leave you here," he said. "Then we'd both feel bad."

August 31, 1845

went up the Creek 5

136

Samuel Parker

Went about five miles this morning and camped once more on Malheur river near a peak in the Blue Mountains called Fremont's peak, the highest point of land in this part of the country, and easily distinguished at a great distance by a large conical rock upon its summit, having one perpendicular side to it. Found an excellent encampment again here.

James Field

Road tolerable good; made an advance of five miles and encamped on a stream affording the best of water; grass and timber in abundance.

Jesse Harritt

June 30, 1989

He appeared on the hill just ahead of me, the sun at his back so I could not see his face. He sat on a big red horse and, in his leisurely way, was "pushing" a white cow across to the other side of the hill where she would be closer to her calf. My approach had scared her off the road and now he'd have to track her down again. "That's all right," he told me. He was about 5'10", but seemed taller because he was uphill and on a horse. He wore blue jeans, a pressed blue shirt, a white cowboy hat and a .22 pistol on his belt. He sat easily and we talked.

"You feel like you're in a can of maggots," he said of western Oregon. "All those cars a-swarming everywhere."

We talked of conservationists: "They want us off the range," he said. "Cattle Free by '93 is their motto. Those Earth Firsters," he shook his head, "They burned down a feedlot in California, just because they didn't like it, I guess. What they don't realize is that ranchers are conservationists, too. I don't know of one who would want to get rid of wildlife. Not one. But, you know, if you don't eat this grass off the wildlife'll just leave, because they don't like it. Or it'd burn."

September 1, 1845

The Worst Road you ever seen 5 wagons Broak Missis Butts
wors

> *Samuel Parker*

Went about five miles, camping again on the Malheur. The road today for short turns, sideling places, hard pulls and jolting stones was rather ahead of anything we have yet had in the same distance, but the camping is first rate.

> *James Field*

Made a small move of five miles over bad road and encamped on the same stream opposite Fremont's Peak, one of the loftiest points of the Blue Mountains; found good grass, and alder timber in abundance.

> *Jesse Harritt*

The "Cattle Free by '93" crowd sees cattlemen as just another tax-subsidized extractive industry, like the timber industry, ripping off the environment and the taxpayer with equal zeal. For instance, according to Denzel and Nancy Ferguson, in Sacred Cows at the Public Trough, between 1963 and 1974 the Bureau of Livestock Management (BLM) spent $20 million to seed about 267,193 acres in the Vale District of Oregon with crested wheat grass. Range improvement expenditures by the BLM over those eleven years totaled $127.6 million in the Vale District. This enormous expense, especially the seeding of the crested wheat grass, was to improve range that would not have needed improvement if it hadn't been severely overgrazed, so, in effect, the BLM rewarded those who wrecked the range for doing so.

In 1983 the Vale District collected about $590,000 in grazing fees. 50% ($295,000) of that amount went back into range improvement—to improve range wrecked by overgrazing. 12.5% ($73,750) went to local governments. Only 37.5% ($221,250) went back to Uncle Sam. If we figured that amount, the $221,250 that went back to Uncle Sam in 1983, as the interest—no payment on principal this year—on only the $20,000,000 paid to spread crested wheat grass over the Vale BLM District, that means that Uncle Sam lent that money to the Vale area ranchers at the mind-boggling interest rate of 1.1%. For the sake of this example we'll just forget the other $107.6 million spent on range improvements in the Vale BLM District over that same time span.

When the seeding project ended in 1974, there were only 235 permittees grazing in the entire district. If each permittee benefitted equally, each would have received about $85,000. But life, and the government, rarely share the good things equally. There were 147 allotments at that time, and 40 of those allotments received nearly all of the $20,000,000. If these 40 allotments were grazed by 65 permittees, each permittee received $307,692.

Cattle on the open public range trample springs and small streams; hasten erosion by compressing soil, removing vegetation and trampling small plants and seedlings; splatter the landscape with excrement (a cow produces about 52 pounds of manure and 20 pounds of urine daily—Ferguson, 57); trample nesting areas of ground-dwelling birds such as the prairie chicken, grouse, killdeer and greater sandhill crane; and overgraze and trample riparian areas and bottomlands. They churn stream bottoms and remove streamside vegetation. Most fish do not thrive in warm, muddy water. Indeed, the cow is an expensive beast, as is the cowboy—but they are our mythology. We need them.

September 2, 1845

139

> *went to A Small Creek down the worst you ever seen A wagon*
> *gow stony 10*
> > Samuel Parker

> *Traveled about 15 miles today, in a direction but little west of*
> *south, camping upon a small branch of the Malheur which puts into*
> *the South Fork. About four miles of our road this morning rather*
> *exceeded anything we have passed over yet for rock, they being both*
> *large and sharp, lying in a narrow ravine where there was no*
> *shunning them. We got through, however, with only one broken*
> *axletree and two wagon tongues, together with some other little*
> *fixings, which was really a favorable come-off.*
> > James Field

> *Made an early start over bad road for three miles; broke one*
> *axletree, which detained us about two hours; balance of the road*
> *tolerable good; traveled 12 miles and encamped on a small rivulet*
> *winding its way through a level valley, with its margin beautifully*
> *adorned with small willows.*
> > Jesse Harritt

I turned east just beyond Bob Browning's ranch, and drove toward Castle Rock, searching for the grave of Sarah King Chambers, who died near Castle Rock on September 3, 1845. Her grave sits on a little knoll overlooking the North Fork of the Malheur.

But I took a wrong turn somewhere. A rocky road serpentined for miles from valley to ridge to valley to ridge, on and on, until I jolted along the lip of an enormous canyon. By then it was late and I camped beneath a couple of junipers high on a windy ridge. Far below, a liquid silver string, the Little Malheur River wended silently seaward. Beyond the Little Malheur, canyon after canyon after canyon rippled off toward the setting sun, etched in the earth's surface like a magnificent and diabolical maze.

The spot I chose was apparently the favorite of an evil-looking brown and white spotted Brahma bull and his harem of a dozen or so Hereford cows. He stood his ground while I lurched off the road, drove across the ridge toward him, toward the trees, until he and the Jeep were almost nose to nose and the cows scattered in all directions. He bellowed and pawed the ground and I got nervous, but he was bluffing. When I revved the engine and beeped the horn, he tossed his head, slung a string of saliva at me, then aimed his shit-splattered rear end my way and kicked up his heels across the sage-covered hilltop.

I dragged out my little aluminum chair, the stove and five-gallon water jug and was just getting comfortable when an old Chevrolet pickup, three dogs in the back, clattered and barked into view. It stopped where the road passed closest to my campsite. The driver climbed out, tossed a beer can into the sagebrush, and pissed, with great relish, relief and volume, on the road. A skinny, gap-toothed fellow leaned from the passenger side window and shouted, "You fishin'?"

"What?"

"Fishing." He parodied a cast with a fly rod.

"Nope." I shouted, shaking my head.

The dogs boiled out of the back of the pickup and began chasing each other through the sagebrush. The passenger climbed out and he, too, pissed on the road. "You can't buy beer," he shouted. "You can only borrow it." Then, beer cans in hand, they stumbled through the sagebrush toward my camp. Thin and muscular and ornery-looking, both about six feet tall, they wore tattooes and beards and ragged Levis, but no shirts. "Shore didn't expect to see you up here," said the darker of the two, extending his hand. "I'm Clyde. This here's Claude."

Clyde's front teeth were gone, leaving a gap in his smile that made him appear demented. "We been up here fifteen days, and you're the first person we've seen." We shook hands, and they grinned and each grasped my hand and held it like they'd found a long-lost friend. A naked lady tattoo undulated on Clyde's forearm

"Yep," said Claude, who stood a little farther away, almost behind his friend.

"What've you been doing up here for 15 days?" I asked.

"Fencin'," came the reply.

"Yep," added Claude.

"You're lookin' at the Rat's Ass Fencing Company," Clyde said. "Thought we'd be finished by now, but last time we went to town we picked up eight more miles."

"Yep, eight more miles," Claude affirmed.

"We're staying right down around the corner," said Clyde. "You're welcome to come on down and join us for dinner."

"Yep, for dinner," said Claude. "I'm a hell of a good cook."

"It's true," said Clyde. "He cooks all our meals and he's a hell of a good cook."

"Yep," said Claude. "Come on down."

"Right around the corner there's a concrete tomb. Some old moonshiner, I think. We're staying in what was probably his camp. Used to be moonshiners all over in these canyons. Dang hard to find."

"Thanks," I said, "but I'm really tired and I just want to go to sleep." I asked if they knew where Sarah King Chambers' grave was. "She was buried in 1845 near where the Meek wagon train crossed the North Fork of the Malheur River," I explained.

"Meek wagon train?" Clyde gave Claude a knowing wink. "You're after the gold, aren't you?"

"Yep, the Blue Bucket Mine," Claude said, rolling his eyes. "We shoulda known."

The Blue Bucket Mine is one of the most enduring legends

of the entire confusing migration, but, until that moment, I hadn't thought much about it. Like most "lost mine" stories, this one has several versions. In the version thought most likely to be true, 21-year-old Dan Herren, who was traveling to Oregon with his aunt and uncle and their 12 children, was trying to round up lost cattle on August 31, 1845, when he picked some shiny rocks from their muddy hoofprints. In another version, the Helm children, playing beside a stream while their mother did the family laundry, gathered shiny rocks from the stream bottom. In another, a woman walking along a stream picked up shiny rocks and carried them in her apron. In all the stories, a blue bucket was filled, or could have been filled, with shiny rocks. Later, when the rocks were used as sinkers on a fishing line, or hammered against a wagonwheel, or used as a door stop, someone realized that they were gold nuggets. Memories were searched and expeditions launched to scour the route of the wagon train, but, to this day, no one has found the lost Blue Bucket Mine.

"Show me the grave of the woman, and I'll show you buckets of gold," said Clyde, grinning. According to the legend, the gold was found one (or two) day's journey west of a woman's grave. Whose grave it is, no one knows for sure, but it is tempting to assume that the grave of Sarah King Chambers is the grave referred to in the legend.

"Yep. I know where the grave of the woman is," said Claude, nodding his head wisely, "and it isn't Sarah Chambers. I know where she is, too."

"And we know where the gold is, too, we think."

"Yep. And you're about 20 miles from Sarah King Chambers' grave. It's near Agency Valley, back that way." Claude pointed back along the road I'd traveled.

"Everybody around here thinks he knows where the gold is," said Clyde, "but nobody's found it yet." They drained the last of the beer and tossed the cans into the sagebrush. By now the Brahma bull had discovered the dogs and he bellowed and pawed the earth while they sniffed and ran around and paid him no attention. "We better get goin'. You're welcome to join us for breakfast in the morning."

"Yep," Claude said. "Come for breakfast. We're having flapjacks." They ambled off toward the middle of the road, where the old pickup sat, doors spraddled open like wings on a wounded duck. The engine caught, the dogs piled in, Clyde and Claude pulled the doors shut, and and the old truck rattled on down the road. The sun's last rays brightened the juniper trees and heightened the gray-green of the sagebrush. Somewhere in the distance Old Man Coyote and his cousins laughed at the departing day. In a little depression just downhill from where I sat, the Brahma bull bellowed and coughed, drawing his harem to him. Then it was quiet, save only the sage-scented wind that forever blows along the Terrible Trail.

September 3, 1845

Stony all day fore miles you codent See the ground 10
Samuel Parker

Went only about six miles today, as we were obliged to put in a new axle-tree. Camped upon the South fork of Malheur again.
It is now pretty evident that Meek, the pilot who is leading the company this route instead of the old one, does not intend to fall down to the Columbia via the John Day river at all as he told them on leaving Fort Boise, for we are evidently now through the Blue Mountains, and still making a south-west course. It is now said that Meek's intention is to take us over onto the head of the Willamette if he can find a place along the Cascades which will admit of the passage of wagons through, and if not we go down the Deschutes river to the Columbia.
James Field

Made new axletree; started late; had good road; traveled seven

miles and encamped on the South Fork (He was mistaken. This is the Middle Fork.) of the Malheur River; found good grass and willows.
    Jesse Harritt

Sarah King Chambers died on September 3, 1845, but, because groups in the wagon train were now separated by a day's travel or more, none of my companions were aware of her death. Also, as James Field mentions above, the immigrants were confused, unsure of Meek's purpose in continuing to head south. When Meek left camp to scout the route ahead, one group decided to kill him. Some favored stoning, others hanging. When he returned, 3 wagons faced each other, tongues lashed together. A noose dangled from the junction of the wagon tongues. Meek escaped hanging, but later, when the death toll continued to climb, he was forced to leave the wagon train.[6]

Midnight? Three a.m.? Warm and damp, like steam, a little cloud sailed by, leaving droplets on my neck and cheek. Some vague, bad feeling about Clyde and Claude had caused me to throw my sleeping bag far out in the sagebrush that night, far from the Jeep and juniper trees. Probably there was nothing to fear, but I felt something sinister in the Rat's Ass Fencing Company and decided to go with my instincts. Might as well make them search if they come for me, I thought.

No moon. Dark as the inside of a cow. Whush! The cloud came again, and, with it, another little shower of droplets. I sat up at the sudden noise, confused by sleep and darkness, and wiped the dampness off my face. Close enough to touch, a large animal bolted, smashing through sage, stumbling over rocks. About twenty feet away, it stopped. Against the sky, I could just make out the silhouette of an enormous, hulking creature. It snorted and stomped and I fumbled for my flashlight. In the feeble yellow beam, two fiendish yellow slits glowed back at me. I felt for a clod or rock and then threw it, hard, at the dark beast. He bellowed and lunged away and I realized then that my antagonist was just the Brahma bull, innocently grazing the night away.

I lay back down, but could not sleep. I was twenty miles from Sarah King Chambers' grave. Might as well get it behind me before sunup, I thought, so I packed up and drove back toward Agency Valley.

September 4, 1845

to A Spring 5
Samuel Parker

Went about 18 miles, the latter part of the road being rough and rocky. Camped upon the head of a small branch of the South fork of the Malheur. The mountains where we first struck them were naked and perfectly destitute of timber. Near Fremont's Peak we began to see some timber upon them, and since passing that point the hills have all had more or less timber upon them, it being generally low cedar, and on reaching the top of the last hill before descending into the hollow, tall pines appear to crown the hill-tops before us.
James Field

Made an advance of 11 miles and encamped in a deep hollow out of which proceeded a number of fine springs, affording us as good water as ever run, with a few small willows.
Jesse Harritt

Deer and "Private Property, Keep Out" signs proliferate in the night. Other signs, too: "Dam fine Hay". I was sleepy, but the signs and locked gates kept me on the road until just below Beulah Dam, where I found a flat space big enough to pull off and roll out my sleeping bag beside the Jeep. I'd just fallen into a sound, dreamless sleep when something—Sam Parker's ghost?

Old May Coyote?—kicked me in the back. I woke up and looked around and heard it retreat up the hill behind me, but even with the gathering light of approaching day I never saw it.

Later, in the bright, clear light of early morning, I woke to the loud, mad cry of a pair of greater sandhill cranes calling across the hayfield on the other side of the road. Plaintive and sad, it echoed off the hillside behind me. Theirs is a cry from another time, the pleistocene, maybe, when the world was more receptive to these magnificent birds. What a privilege it is to hear them today. I lay on my back, turned my ear to Nature and heard also the meadowlark's sweet, assertive song; the callous chatter of a tribe of blackbirds; the thrum of a flicker on a juniper trunk; the whine of a mosquito, more of a drone here, the mosquitoes being bigger and slower; the buzz of big bees in the juniper trees; and the soft, sibilant wind in the sage.

September 5, 1845

Crossed the Divide to the head waters of the digers lakes in the nite 11 oclock 23
Samuel Parker

Went 15 miles, camping upon the Lake fork of John Day's River. I was mistaken about our being through the Blue Mountains. Although we were through the main range, yet the road for the past few days has led across low mountains which, having their steepest descent toward the west, did not appear high until we ascended them. The map of the country we had with us also indicated that we had passed the head of the John Day river, as the Malheur was made to head much further south than the John Day, and yet we have held a south south-west course from the Malheur, and are now upon the head forks of the John Day river.
James Field

As we advanced we gradually ascended a beautiful mountain; gained the top, upon which grew a number of pine and cedar trees; a few miles further a beautiful landscape appeared to sight. To the west a large valley, to the southwest the Cascade Mountains; to the northwest was the Columbia River. We gradually descended this lofty mountain, entered the valley, down which we proceeded five miles; came to a beautiful little rivulet with its banks shaded by a few small willows, where we encamped, having come 12 miles.
    Jesse Harritt

An hour or so later, Stanton Joad threw a saddle over a tall, red mare and looked toward the road where he saw my little green Jeep hesitate and then plunge down his driveway. Still looking for the grave of Sarah King Chambers, I came to ask for directions. The horse, tethered to the tailgate of an old Ford pickup, nickered quietly and sidestepped as I pulled slowly by to park where the driveway widened to a turn-around and parking area in front of a white trailerhouse. Cattle grazed in the meadows on both sides of the trailer and a line of willow trees ran along the bank of the North Fork of the Malheur River about a hundred feet behind the trailer.

Pale blue eyes inspected me from beneath the wide, droopy brim of a big black cowboy hat as I stepped from the Jeep. "Howdy." He sounded wary, suspicious. A heavy, black moustache pulled his face into a frown. As he stepped away from the horse I felt for an instant as if I'd stepped back in time, that I might be confronting Bat Masterson saddling up to gallop down the road and rob a stagecoach. "What can I do for you?" he growled.

"I'm trying to follow the trail of a wagon train that passed through here in 1845," I said, "and I'm looking for the grave of Sarah King Chambers, who died just before the wagon train crossed the North Fork of the Malheur River. I wondered if you had any idea where that grave might be."

"I think I know where it is. My mom showed me that grave when I was a kid. Are you a historian?"

"In a way," I told him, "but mainly I'm just a writer trying to follow the trail and write a story about it."

"You been running into lots of 'Private Property' and 'No Trespassing' signs?" he asked. Then, before I could answer: "Where're you from?"

"Eugene," I said, answering the last question first. "Private property signs, fences, locked gates everywhere. It's a lot different now from when I was a kid," I told him, "harder to find a camping spot now than it was even last spring." I told him of the trouble I'd had locating a spot to pull off the road in the dark, that I'd slept just a couple of miles away about 20 feet from the road.

At this information, his eyes seemed to light up and a serious grin creased his face. "We're fighting that goddamn..." He leveled an accusing gaze at me. "You probably voted for it!" His voice rose a few decibels and he stepped toward me. "That goddamn Wild and Scenic Rivers Act."

"Well, yeah," I admitted. "I thought it was a good piece of legislation. I even stood in front of a grocery store and gathered signatures to place it on the ballot."

"THEM SONSABITCHES..." he shouted, waving his right forefinger in the air like a politician on the stump. "That's a terrible law. Them sonsabitches can come right in here and condemn property that's been family farms for over a hundred years. Them sonsabitches have to get in to inspect it first, though," he grinned, "and we won't give 'em permission to cross onto our private property."

"Condemn family farms..?" I started to ask, puzzled.

"That's right," he shouted, stepping closer and aiming his forefinger at my chest like a pistol. "Them sonsabitches can take away our grazing rights, even though they they're grandfathered in..."

149

"Wait, wait..." I protested, holding my hands up defensively. "Are we talking about the same law? The Wild and Scenic Rivers Act I voted for was to protect designated significant rivers from mining and clearcutting. It's a good law that protects fisheries and riparian areas..."

"Riparian areas!" he snorted, stepping so close now that I could feel his breath as each word burst into the air. We are about the same size, that is, about 5'10", 190 pounds. He advanced and I stubbornly refused to retreat. We stood, nose to nose, and our discussion continued, each sentence louder than the one before. "Riparian areas... Now you're talking about range management, and who knows more about range management than the families who've been managing the range for more than a hundred years? Cows build and help maintain riparian areas by breaking down stream banks..."

"Bullshit," I said, "That's simply untrue." It hit him like a rifle shot and he stopped mid-tirade, calloused finger upraised. "Cows," I said, trying to sound calm and knowledgable, "trample springs and riparian areas clear out of existence. They eat streamside vegetation, removing plants that shade the water, causing the water temperature to rise. They trample stream banks, muddy the water, and cause spawning beds to silt up. Cow manure and urine pollute streams and rivers. The cow and the fish are not friends."

"I want you to read some stuff about that law," he said, wrenching the pickup door open. He rustled around in a pile of papers on the floor of the cab and came up with a handful of livestock industry publications. "Here," he said, thrusting them at me. "Read these and you'll see what a bad law you helped pass. In this one," he pulled a Nevada publication from the stack, "there's a letter I wrote." The note of pride in his voice at having been published was unmistakable. I took the stack of papers and promised to read them later.

"You said you thought you knew where that grave might

be," I reminded him.

"What're you doing out here in the middle of the week?" he asked. "Don't you have a job?"

"I'm a teacher most of the time. This is my summer vacation."

"You probably make $30,000 a year." He shook his head in disbelief. "We get lots of government people out here looking around on the taxpayer's time."

"I'm on my own time," I assured him.

"I give range tours," he said, "as a range consultant, explaining basic ranching principles and range management principles. I charge $500 a day per person. They have to bring their own lunch and a pair of gum boots to cross the river. The tours are nothing fancy, just plain common sense."

"Five hundred dollars a day? Are you kidding?"

"I'm not kidding. But I will not take on tour any local or federal government workers unless they can prove they are on their own time and expense. And it will have to be able to stand up to a Freedom of Information check, so you and I as taxpayers will not have to foot the bill. Same with teachers. They must be on their own time and expense."

"Five hundred dollars a day is even more than an English teacher makes," I told him. "This tour business sounds like a pretty good racket. Tell you what," I grinned, "for $500 a day I'll take on tour all those government workers and teachers who get the government to pay their way. No sense discriminating against those folks."

He was not amused. "You probably believe in abortion," he charged, his eyes narrowing.

"Well, it's not so much that I believe in abortion as that I don't believe I have the right to make that kind of a choice for another person."

"Abortion is murder," he shot back.

"What do your daughters think about this? I asked.

"I don't have any daughters."

"Well, then, what does your wife think about it?" I asked.

"I'm not married," he answered.

"Your girlfriend?"

"Don't have a girlfriend."

"Any sisters?"

"No. What's this?" Unconsciously, we'd begun to circle each other, like verbal boxers sparring, and our match had taken us across the parking area to where we now leaned against the back of the Jeep. He pointed at my 'Hayduke Lives' bumper sticker. "Earth First!?" He read the fine print along the bottom that identified Earth First! as the originator of the bumper sticker, then spit out the words like a mouthful of sour milk. "Them sonsabitches burned down a stockyard in California last week. You aren't one of them, are you?"

"No," I said, "I don't belong to Earth First!, but I sympathize with their activities, especially when it comes to saving ancient forests."

"I just hope some rancher around here doesn't get hotheaded and gut-shoot some of these terrorists. A partial job would surely get him in trouble with his neighbors." He smiled, "You'd better not drive around here with that written on your car. Besides being bad manners, it's probably dangerous."

With my pocket knife I sliced the bottom of the bumpersticker, then peeled the offending line of print from the bumper. I rolled it into a little ball and handed it to him. "Here," I said. "Now I'm safe." He dropped it into the dirt.

"What's this mean, 'Hayduke Lives'?"

"Hayduke's a character in a book called The Monkeywrench Gang," I explained. "You should read it."

"Well, I guess you're safe with just that on there," he said. "Most people around here won't know who Hayduke is. Now, that grave you asked about..."

Two hours passed between our first word and our last. The horse waited patiently, half saddled, tethered to the back of the pickup. We exchanged names, addresses, handshakes, and, though we disagreed on almost every topic, we retained a measure of respect and fondness for one another. "You haven't heard the last from me," he shouted as I drove away. Indeed, I hope not.

Half an hour later, I stood near the grave of Sarah King Chambers. Enclosed now in a little pen of hogwire, the gravestone is set upright in concrete. On it, less legible each year, is scratched, "S. Chambers, Sept. 3, 1845". I stood in the sun and tried to imagine the somber crowd of pioneers gathered here that day, but a truck rumbled by on the road just below and a heavy, four-engine, propeller-driven airplane roared overhead, shattering my reverie.

The river here runs southeast. Due west, the land rises and falls in a series of valleys, canyons, gulleys and gulches, too formidable a challenge even for a Jeep, so it is hard to imagine that 200 wagons would travel that direction. Instead, they continued northwest, up the North Fork of the Malheur to where they could climb up and out of the canyon, turn gradually west and then southwest, down Cottonwood Creek to its junctions with Warm Springs Creek and Otis Creek and into the Drewsey Valley, where they once again encountered the Malheur River. They then crossed the Stinkingwater Mountains, descended into Pine Creek, then to the head of Big Rock Creek, and found their way into Harney Valley by way of East Cow Creek. In Fred Lockley's column, "Impressions and Observations of the Journal Man", dated September 13, 1924, C. A. Sweek tells of the tracks of the wagon train still visible down Cow Creek in that year.

September 6, 1845

153

down the Botom Sandy and Sage 23
Samuel Parker

Went about 14 miles today, camping upon another fork of Crooked river instead of John Day as stated yesterday, and we are in fact upon the waters of Deschutes river, and steering direct toward the Cascade mountains in order to attempt a passage through them.

The tale of our going down the John Day river was a mere tale of Meek's in order to get us upon this route and then take us wherever he pleased. But if he now fails to take us across the Cascades his head will not be worth a chew of tobacco to him, if what some of our men say prove true. He is with Owensby's company, which is one day's travel ahead of ours, and we make their camps ever evening, where we find a note buried at the foot of a stake, stating the distance to the next camp, and the names of the streams.

James Field

Continued down this rich valley 14 miles and encamped on Crooked River (Silvies River), a small murmuring stream running to the south, shaded on its banks by a few willows.

As we advanced this morning the beautiful scenery increased. This valley is one of the most sublime places I ever saw; it is from appearance from 30 to 50 miles wide from north to south the length of which I am not able to determine' the soil is rich and beautifully set over with fine grass intermixed with patches of sage; the mountains to the north in places are thickly set with pine and cedar (juniper) timber.

Jesse Harritt

The indigenous people of this area were Warm Springs Indians, but they were called Digger Indians or Diggers by the immigrants. They were scavengers, insect-eaters. The immigrants considered them very primitive.

I came to the headwaters of the "digers lakes" and then

into Harney Valley and the lakes themselves—Malheur Lake and Harney Lake—by a slightly different route, one dictated by fences and roads, Private Property signs and locked gates. From Sarah Chambers' grave I drove northwest, then south, and eventually found the village of Drewsey, once again near Highway 20. From there it was nearly a straight shot west almost to Burns, then south to rejoin the trail just north of Malheur Lake.

September 7, 1845

Struck the lakes Bad water 22
Samuel Parker

Went about 16 miles, camping upon a lake of miserable, stagnant water, filled with ducks, geese and cranes, and surrounded with tall rushes, the borders being miry. Had excellent grass, but were obliged to pack wormwood for half a mile for fuel. During the night 15 head of horses and mules left us.
James Field

Road beautiful and level; traveled 16 miles; crossed one small stream and encamped on the northern margin of a large lake (Malheur Lake); had an abundance of fine grass; no wood except sage.
Jesse Harritt

My companions traveled around the east end of Wright's Point, a long, flat-topped hill that runs like a wall along the southern horizon, then turned west along the north shore of Harney Lake. As I approached Wright's Point from the north on Highway 205, I could see them among the other mirages, plodding westward through the afternoon heat. In 1833, Stephen Meek trapped here, along the shore of a magnificent lake. Because Harney and Malheur Lakes have no outlet to the sea, their water levels rise and fall with the relative amounts of precipitation and evaporation. In 1845, after a series of drought years, the lake had shrunk to a pond of "miserable, stagnant water." The confidence of the immigrants and Meek's confidence in himself here sank to an all-time low. In 1867, after a few years of higher-than-normal precipitation, Meek returned to find the magnificent lake where it had been in 1833. In 1988 and 1989 the lakes were again at a high level, but a year of drought had shrunk them considerably by the summer of 1990.

Highway 205 jogs diagonally up the wall of Wright's Point, then plummets down the south side. A county road appears to skirt the north shore of Harney Lake, running west along the approximate route of the wagon train. Thinking I was back on the trail again, I turned west along the county road.

September 8, 1845
went down the lakes some 5 miles then over hills to A Small Creek one child buried here 15
        Samuel Parker

Went about 13 miles, camping upon a creek which appears to feed the lake our last camp was situated upon. We have been traveling for the last three days across a nearly dead level plain, in a southwesterly direction, and are now nearly across it, the bluffs rising abruptly from the level of the plain, which they surround, and are in many places nearly perpendicular.

Many parts of this plain, particularly where we struck it, has a soil of good depth, and is covered with a very find kind of grass resembling blue grass. Much of it is covered with that same eternal wormwood mentioned so often, and there are many places which look as though they were covered with water during the wet season, now presenting a surface of naked white clay encrusted in place with a white substance resembling saleratus and answering the same purpose, as some of the women in camp have proven by experiment.

Four of the horses which left our last camp were found to-day at

a distance of several miles from it, but there is no news of the others.
They probably strayed off in search of water, as the borders of the lake
were so miry they could not get a drink.
     James Field

Road continues delightful; had 10 horses stolen last night by the
Indians. travel 10 miles and encamped on a small stream (Silvies
River) affording good grass and a few small willows. A dreadful
occurrence a few minutes after we were in camp—sudden death of one
infant by that disease which has been fatal before in our company,—
the whooping cough.
     Jesse Harritt

Death visited the wagon train frequently now, with little
children and the elderly its first and most frequent victims.

               September 9, 1845

   went to A Spring
   Samuel Parker

Last evening a child of E. Packwood, of Illinois, which had been
ill a few days died suddenly. At present there are a good many sick
about the camp, the majority of them complaining of fever.
   The child was buried in the dry wormwood barrens, and as we
left the camp the wagons filed out over the grave, thus leaving no trace
of its situation. The reason of our doing this was that the Indians in
this part of the country are very fond of clothing, giving almost
anything they possess in order to obtain it, and fearing that they might
disturb the grave after we left, we took the precaution of leaving a
beaten road across it. I cannot say that they would do anything to a
grave were they to find one, for we have passed several evidently made
by the emigrants at various times, and none of them appeared to have
been disturbed.
   Went six miles, camping near a spring which sinks near where

it rises.

> James Field

Attended to the burial of the deceased this morning before we started; made a start at 10 o'clock; traveled six miles over a delightful road and encamped at a spring; found no wood, and but little grass.

> Jesse Harritt

I zipped along the county road toward Silver Lake, imagining the sad, disillusioned members of the wagon train, their numbers dwindling daily, each day's camp routine now including the burial of their dead. The Packwood child was buried on the west shore of Silver Lake, near Crane Spring. I knew there would be no visible reminder of that grim event, but I wanted to visit the site of the burial, to put the event in its proper physical context.

An emaciated, acne-stricken teenager in a little red pickup waved me down as I topped a hill near the north shore of Harney Lake, about 10 miles west of Highway 205. His head, half swallowed by a cowboy hat that just barely fit into the pickup cab, appeared shrunken. His eyes, too big for his small face, bulged, seemed to strain to see from beneath the great brim. "Where you goin'?"

"Over there," I said, pointing west. "Silver Lake, then Wagontire, if I can find a way through."

"This here's private property," he said, nervously. "You can't go through here."

"This is a county road," I told him. "Surely the public has access through here."

"Nope."

"So, how can I get to Silver Lake?" I asked.

"Can't. Private property."

"How do I get out of here?" I asked, not wanting to hear the answer.

"Go back the way you came."

"That's ten or 15 miles back to the highway," I whined.

"Sorry. My boss don't want no one driving through here."

"What's he growing over there? Marijuana?"

"Gosh, no," he giggled. "Hay."

With a rare (for me) show of good behavior that I've regretted ever since, I turned and obediently headed back the way I'd come. My companions may have had a rough time in 1845, but they didn't have to deal with locked gates, barbed-wire fences, roads and access to private property. At times I felt that I'd be happy to trade them problems.

September 10, 1845

went all day and all nite and struck A small Spring in the morning Cursing and Swareing 105 wagons together 40
Samuel Parker

The ground about our encampment is encrusted with salt, which in some places may be scraped up with the hand in nearly a pure state. Went about 30 miles today, over a road pretty well strewn with the hard, round nigger-heads frequently mentioned after leaving Fort Hall, and camped after midnight at a spring, where we found Owensby's company, which had arrived 24 hours before us. Their last camp was about seven miles this side of ours, and it was a dry one in the midst of wormwood barrens, so that they were nearly two days without water. We found about 100 head of their stock between the two encampments, apparently nearly famished for water, and drove them on with us, but few of them giving out on the way, although they looked miserable.
James Field

Made a late start; traveled a west course over a tolerable level road, though very stony in places; found no grass nor water for 25 miles; at one o'clock this morning we gradually descended a long

slope; found a good spring affording an abundance of water, and grass, with a few willows (Leaving Silvies River Valley).
   Jesse Harritt

   I decided to intersect the route at Wagontire, due west of Harney Lake, but to get there I had to drive east to Highway 205, north to Highway 20, west to Highway 395, and south to Wagontire—outlining an 85 mile square to cover the next 25 miles of trail.

September 11, 1845
to Another Spring   5   laid heare 4 days and some five days Codent find now water frome 10 to 20 and 30 men out hunting water Some Came in to Camp and Codent Speek Water found
   Samuel Parker

   It being 2 o'clock this morning before we got to camp, we stuck to it the remainder of the day. Owensby's company left about noon for a camp six or seven miles ahead. His company are in as much confusion as any set of fellows I have seen on the road. Having lost confidence in Meek, many of them are trying to hunt a road for themselves.
   It seems there was a misunderstanding between us and Meek when we left Snake river respecting the route he intended taking. We understood him that on leaving the Malheur river he intended striking over to the John Day river and down it to the old road. When we found ourselves on the branches of the Deschutes river it rather surprised us, and as we had a report in camp a few days before that he was going to pilot Owensby across the Cascade mountains to the Willamette settlements, we supposed he was taking a straight shoot for them. It seems that he calls the Deschutes river the John Jay, which he says is the name by which it is known to the mountain traders, and the similarity in the sound of the two names made us mistake the one for the other.

160

It was his intention to follow down Crooked river to Deschutes and down it to the old road, but when he came to the marshy lake spoken of last Sunday, the company refused to follow him if he made the circuit necessary to get around it upon Crooked river again so he struck off in a westerly direction in order to get upon the main Deschutes river. He well knew that there was a scarcity of both grass and water across here and so informed them, but it was nearer and they would have him go it, and now blame him for coming the route they obliged him to.
James Field

Laid by all day to rest our teams.
Jesse Harritt

West of Burns the wormwood barrens roll on and on for miles. One of the groups of wagon trains is said to have camped near here in sagebrush higher than the wagons. This is one of my favorite places, and, as it was late in the day when I arrived, I stopped for the night. Miles from the nearest person, it was a night of shooting stars, satellites, and stars spangling the sky after a wonderful orange sunset. Coyotes laughed madly and I slept soundly.

July 1, 1989
Sitting on my little chair at 6:45 a.m. All that sky, all that land, miles and miles that I can see and I'm the only one enjoying it. Sipping coffee, warmed by the sun like a snake on the road. Not even many birds here. A coyote or two in the distance, squaw Butte to the southwest. Not quite on the Terrible Trail. Sweet, clean air, sage, bunchgrass, juniper.

I wonder what my companions would think of this manner of travel. Maybe they'd envy it, but maybe not. Coffee in flakes, water boiling over a little butane stove, like magic. And my mechanical mule. Why'd I ever want to walk this route, anyway? Even they didn't walk it. They might prefer horseback, but it's hard to beat a Jeep. Food in Ziploc bags. Sanitary, convenient, might have cut down the death toll. Just add water and—ugh!—a barely palatable gruel. Ya gotta be hungry. They'd like this little chair of plastic and aluminum. It'd keep them from sitting in the dirt.

Speaking of dirt, dust coats everything—in my eyes, in my mouth...

Wagontire Mountain, about 25 miles due west of Silver Lake, was a sad place in September, 1845. On the mountain's northwest side is Lost Creek Spring, in a place known to my companions as Lost Hollow. This was the last water, the end of their tether, the place they had to stop until water was found farther along the trail. Some families were so low on food that they salted grass and ate it. They did not have enough food to turn back, and they didn't have enough food to waste time waiting around Lost Hollow. What water there was was insufficient for the influx of people and animals, but there was some, so there they waited, sending out party after party to search for water.

In the spring of 1989, I explored Wagontire Mountain, coming from the west to eventually find my way down to Highway 395 near Wagontire. Driving up one particularly bumpy road near what I assumed was Lost Hollow, I reached with my foot for the clutch and found it flat on the floor. When I stopped and crawled under the Jeep to investigate, I found that a part of the clutch linkage, had fallen out. I tried to replace the missing part by carving a replica from a juniper branch, but I couldn't get it quite right. I was miles from help and had no clutch. Then I remembered an art I had acquired years before as a teen-age pea truck driver. It was a forbidden art, but I had learned it just the same—at the cost, probably, of a truck transmission or two for my employer, the Irvin Mann Ranch. I had once been able to drive a truck without using the clutch. Probably any teenage truck driver can. I hadn't tried it for years, but there are some things you just don't forget. I drove on to Burns, stopping to open and close innumerable gates, shifting gears smoothly, by ear, without a clutch. No one in Burns had the correct part, but, with help from a clerk in an auto parts store, I pieced together a replacement that works better than the original.

Today, coming from the east, a fence runs like a wall for miles along the east slope of the mountain, blocking access, at least from this side, to Lost Hollow. On the gate through which I passed last spring hangs a new chain and padlock.

Thirsty and frustrated, I stopped in the Wagontire Store for a drink of something cold and wet. I bellied up to the bar and ordered a tall, cool, Coke. While I sat there sipping the Coke and crunching the ice cubes and wiping the little drips of condensation from the outside of the glass onto my cheeks, the barmaid, a thin, old lady with spectacles and a face like a librarian, eyed me suspiciously. "You look awful hot," she said.

"You should have seen me a few days ago," I answered, thinking of the hell-trek to Vale. I asked if she knew how to get to Wagontire Mountain, but she knew nothing of the fence or the locks or where there might be an unlocked gate. "Did you ever hear anything about the Meek wagon train?" I asked. "Came through here in 1845."

Her eyes lit up and she moved closer, placing her elbows on the bar opposite me. "Why, yes," she said, nodding. "Certainly. That's how Wagontire got its name. The Meek wagon train came through here and the Indians attacked and killed 'em all. Burned all the wagons. Only thing left was a wagon-tire."

September 12, 1845
Went about six miles, camping upon another little spring (illegible) running a short distance sinks again. The ravine looks as though a smart branch ran through it at some seasons of the year. The hills around are covered with cedars; with the exception of a plain to

westward, that appears to be the case with all the country to the north and west of us, as far as the eye can reach, and that appears to be to the Cascade mountains. Found two-thirds of Owensby's company still here, the remainder having gone on with the pilot and captain. A party of five men who left us last Tuesday morning to go back in search of the missing horses returned tonight bringing in nine of them which they had taken from a party of Indians, near Crooked river. The Indians appeared loth to give them up but they charged upon them and took them, running the Indians off, who they say are a miserable set of wretches with no arms but bows and arrows.

    James Field

Made a small move of five miles and encamped on a small branch; found tolerable grass and cedar timber in abundance.

    Jesse Harritt

September 13, 1845

Started this morning in expectation of a long drive across the plain before us, but when about four miles from camp met Meek's wife in company with a friend, returning with the news that they had found no water as yet and requesting all who were at the spring to remain there until he found a camp and returned or sent word back for them to come on. Nothing remained for us to do but drive back to the camp we had just left where we found Tethero's company also, so if misery loves company here is enough of it, for this small camping spot is nearly eaten out by our own large stock of cattle and to add to all this there are some in the company nearly out of provisions.

    James Field

Made a start; traveled three miles, met the men who had accompanied the pilot (Meek) in search of water; found none; we returned to our old encampment and stopped for the night.

    Jesse Harritt

Meek was not immune to thirst, but he may have known

more ways to avoid it than the immigrants he was leading: "One of Meek's tricks, learned in the hard school of necessity, stood him in good stead on the 1845 crossing. Unable to get to water, Meek opened a vein in the neck of his mule and drank the blood, thus averting death from thirst."[7]

September 14, 1845
Last evening the portion of Owensby's company which were out upon the plain returned with their cattle and water kegs, having left their wagons out upon the plain seven miles from here and no water had then been found within 30 miles of them. To-day Meek ordered them to return to this place and sent an order for us to remain at this place until tomorrow morning, then let 10 or 12 men accompany him with spades and dig for water at a place he thinks it can be found, in the dry bed of a creek.

This evening Owensby returned with his wagons, teams, cattle, and all, having enough of lying out in the plain upon uncertainties. Meek came in after dark and said that from the top of a mountain a short distance from here he had discovered a cut in the side of a mountain apparently 15 miles distant where from the bright green appearance of the willows and grass there could be no doubt of our finding water and requesting that some horsemen might accompany him to search the mountain sides still further; he thought there would be no danger in some wagons starting tomorrow.
James Field

Laid still all day waiting the return of the pilot; he returned late in the evening; found no water.
Jesse Harritt

Scouts searched for miles to the west and to the north but found no water. Morning ice and frost told the immigrants winter was not far off. As they could not move on without water and they hadn't enough food to stay or return, they apparently had to choose between dying of thirst in the desert and freezing to death or dying of starvation or dysentery or another communicable disease at Lost Hollow.

September 15, 1845

This afternoon about three o'clock, 21 of Tetherow's wagons, together with six or seven of Owensby's company, made a start for the spot spoken of yesterday, which lies northeasterly from here, Meek accompanying them. A company of eight or ten wagons passed through the hollow we are encamped in, and started out into the plains by moonlight in the evening. They were a company we had never seen before and they said they were the last to leave the States for Oregon this year, starting some two or three weeks behind us. Their loose stock were nearly all working steers, they having enough apparently to change teams every day.
　　James Field

Dispatched a company of men with their pack horses loaded with water and provision in search of water.
　　Jesse Harritt

A meeting was held to seek a solution. Much shouting and stomping and cursing followed, but no solution was presented, so they decided once again to hang Stephen Meek.

Just as the meeting broke up, Meek arrived with good news. He had seen a green hillside to the north and thought there would be water there. "...the excitement was intense, and famine seemed inevitable. The feelings of our company towards the guide were of that unmistakable character to justify me in telling him his life was in danger; his reply was, "I have known it for several days, but what can I do? I have brought you here, and will take you off, if you will go."[8]

The immigrants felt that anything was better than another day at Lost Hollow, so they immediately sent scouts north to search for water. Apparently the promise of water drained them of their resolve to punish Meek, and he once again escaped the noose.

September 16, 1845
left at 3 p m oclock traveled all nite come to water at Sunrise 30 Missis Butts now betor (no better) 198 wagons in Company 2,299 loose Cattle oxen 811 head all thes Cattle to git water and 1051 Gotes also consume A heap of water
Samuel Parker

Capt. Riggs accompanied by the two Wilcoxs' started yesterday morning to search for water at a place they had seen the day before, and which the description given by Meek of the spot he expected to find water at, applied to precisely. They returned this morning reporting it the same with plenty of water and grass.

We made preparation for starting immediately, but could not get ready until late in the afternoon, as our cattle were so scattered. We had a clear, full moon to light us on our toilsome way, which lay across a mountain to the northward, and after traveling about 20 miles we reached the long-sought spot at daybreak.
James Field

The hunters returned this morning at nine o'clock; found water in 25 miles; in a few minutes the companies were in parade for their oxen, made a general collection of stock; between four l'clock and sundown about 80 wagons left the branch for the next encampment; travel all night.

At daybreak we reached the place of encampment at a small mountain stream (headwaters of Crooked River) winding its way through a level valley; found no wood except sage which grew in abundance near its margin; having come 25 miles, we stopped to take some refreshment and rest our teams.
Jesse Harritt

They traveled all night beneath the cool light of a full moon, the lead companies building bonfires every two or three miles to serve as beacons for those following. They found water at a place now called GI Ranch, on the south fork of Crooked River. Meek must have had trouble not saying, "I told you so," because, had they traveled the trail he preferred, they would have arrived at GI Ranch a week earlier and now be much farther down the trail to The Dalles.

Here, in September, 1845, the wagon train split. The South Fork of the Crooked River flowed north, apparently to the Columbia River, but Meek thought the best route north lay still farther west and that was the direction he intended to travel. About 33 wagons, including those belonging to William Helm and Solomon Tetherow and their families, headed west. The rest, including Samuel Parker, Jesse Harritt, and James Field, traveled north and then west.

Near here, in July, 1989, I could see the Cascades, and knew that just on the other side, about 3 hours away by Jeep, my family, lemonade, shade, and baseball games awaited. Confined even more now by roads and fences, the Terrible Trail lost much of its attractiveness. The pull of summertime activities in the Willamette Valley was strong. With the thought that I'd finish the trail another time, I headed home.

My daughter, Polly, and I picked up the trail again at GI Ranch in July, 1990. In spite of the fierce desert heat, sagebrush and grass were green for miles around. We traveled west along a dirt track, trying to approximate the wagon route. Antelope and deer browsed nonchalantly as we passed, fat partridges waddled along the road, jackrabbits bounced through the sagebrush, and two enormous elk rose from their afternoon naps to bound like horses down the road in front of our Jeep. Later, the full moon shone on the desert floor—"like a spotlight," Polly said—and we imagined the wagon train proceeding anxiously, resolutely, in the light of the desert night, to the promise of water at GI Ranch. We slept in a gully high above a seasonal creek, beneath juniper trees old enough to have sheltered the immigrants of 1845. As we drifted off to sleep, porcupines shuffled into the juniper trees and an owl called to us from somewhere down the creek. Off in the distance, Old Man Coyote sang his mad song.

The westbound portion of the train stopped to bury a child, whose body was placed in a trunk before burial, and eat dinner near the northwest end of Hampton Butte. They then traveled all night, across Pringle Flatt, down Ant Creek to Bear Creek, then up Spring Creek and camped at a spring south of Little Bear Creek.

Some of the confusing pieces of the Blue Bucket Mine puzzle may have originated here. Reverend Helm told of needing weights for fishing line and said he found glittering pieces of metal and pounded them into weights. Isaac Butler said that, from the place where the gold was, he could see a big landslide on the slope of the Cascades. In another story, a woman died here. Apparently no one recorded her name, only that her grave was heaped with glittering rocks. "Show me the grave of the woman and I'll show you buckets of gold."

September 17, 1845

went to A creek 11
Samuel Parker

We are now nearer or as near the spring from which we made the 30-mile stretch on the 10th inst. as at the camp after we had made it and this too after lying in vexatious suspense, cramped in a little narrow, barren, rocky hollow among the mountains, with the dry plain some 40 or 50 miles in extent before us with the delightful anticipation that we would be obliged to cross it before reaching water.

Nor was this all; more than one family had shaken the last flour from their sack, and others could calculate to a certainty the day they

would do likewise. Lay by today wishing to get a smaller company if possible, three large ones being mixed together.
    James Field

After taking some refreshment we yoked our teams at two o'clock p.m.; traveled six miles and encamped on Sandy (Crooked River), a delightful stream running to the northwest, affording an abundance of fine grass; no wood.
    Jesse Harritt

As the ordeal wore on, tempers grew shorter and shorter. Stephen Meek's life was never out of danger. Years later, in an interview with Fred Lockley, Susannah Peterson, who traveled with Tetherow, Helm and Meek in the westbound portion of the wagon train, remembered, while ascending a "powerful steep place" —probably near the Maury Mountains—that:

One of the men that happened to be just ahead of us said: "When I get to the top of this hill, if I ever do, I am going to hunt for Stephen Meek and if I find him, I'll kill him!"
Meek was sitting just above us, back of a big sagebrush. He stepped out with his gun in his hand and said, awful slow and cool, "Well, you've found me, go ahead with the killing!"
The man wilted down and didn't have spunk enough to kill a prairie dog. He was like a lot of other bad men—just a bad man with his mouth.[9]

September 18, 1845
Three miles down we crossed over to the west side and after a travel of 12 miles we encamped at a good spring; found good grass and some cedar timber.
    Jesse Harritt

I

over hills and Rock all day Come down A Steep hill got water

15

Samuel Parker

Traveled about 11 miles in a northwesterly direction, striking a smart-sized creek running in the same direction and camping upon it. This creek has no brush upon its banks, which was the reason of it being overlooked when they searched the country for water.

It is evident that Meek's knowledge of the country has rather failed him here, since it is actually a shorter drive from the spring we left on the 10th inst. to the head of the branch we camped upon yesterday than it is from the 10th to the 11th, and apparently a better road. Had we taken that road we would now be advanced at least 80 miles upon our journey, besides being saved the trying suspense of remaining in a miserable encampment several days, with no prospect of water ahead for forty or fifty miles.

James Field

On September 18, Stephen Meek and Solomon Tetherow followed an Indian to the top of a high hill, probably Alkali Butte, a few miles southeast of what is now Prineville Reservoir. From there they could see the valleys of the Deschutes and Crooked Rivers and the peaks of the Cascades. The Indian told them that The Dalles was about five days journey, that they should go west and then turn north, that they would find water near Powell Buttes, about ten miles southwest of Prineville.

September 19, 1845
down the Creek some times in and some times out 7
Samuel Parker

Made an advance of 12 miles and encamped again on Sandy; found grass and a few small willows.

Jesse Harritt

Went about 22 miles, road tolerably rough much of the way, camping upon a stream in a deep, narrow glen resembling the Malheur much in character, and which we believe to be Lohum's fork of Deschutes or Falls river.
James Field

Tetherow's group sent out two advance parties on September 19. One group headed north, toward Pilot Butte, for The Dalles, seeking help. They took with them four days' supplies, planning to eat at The Dalles on the fifth day. The other group went west to search for a pass through the Cascades. The main group traveled west, across Alkali Flats, and camped near Bear Creek.

September 20, 1845
dow(n) the same Cree (k) in and out 10
Samuel Parker

Went about eight miles, camping upon the same stream mentioned yesterday, down which we followed all day, frequently crossing it, and at one narrow pass we were obliged to follow the bed of the river for nearly a fourth of a mile.
James Field

Continued down the creek; passed through several narrow avenues where the mountains closed in on both sides, where we were compelled to follow down the channel of the creek for several hundred yards in water up to our wagon beds; continued to follow its meanders, crossing its channel a number of times; after an advance of 13 miles we encamped; found grass and willows.
Jesse Harritt

The main group traveled down Camp Creek Valley, along the east side of Maury Mountains, and entered the Crooked River Valley 3/4 mile west of Camp Creek.

Tetherow's group traveled twelve miles on the 20th, and camped near Alfalfa. They buried two people here: an unknown person whose grave was marked by a tree limb on which was carved, "Sacred to the memorie of Je....ie", and a 13-year-old girl, Elisa Harris.

September 21, 1845

left the Creek 2 miles up the Same some of the company dident git up till after dark went 4 miles to A Small Spring 6 Swareing without end Comeing in all nite
    Samuel Parker

Went about 16 miles today, still keeping down the river, occasionally cutting across the lowest points of the bluffs, and camping upon it again. The hills along the stream upon either hand are covered in many places with tall pines.
    James Field

Down the creek 10 miles; Had bad road; we encamped; found grass, willow and cedar timber in abundance.
    Jesse Harritt

The scouts returned to Tetherow's group from the Cascades on the 21st. They were unable to find a route through to the Willamette Valley, so the immigrants decided to press on, north, to The Dalles.

September 22, 1845

to A Creek 19
    Samuel Parker

Went about seven miles, keeping still down along the river, which has to be crossed every mile or two, and sometimes two or three times in a mile. Camped at the foot of a tremendous hill, which it is necessary to ascend, and which when we first came in sight of appeared to be strung with wagons from the bottom to near the top, several companies being engaged in the ascent at the same time.

James Field

Three miles brought us to the foot of a huge mountain, (Ascent from Crooked River Valley to the plateau to the north, about five miles west of Prineville.) where we commenced ascending through thick cedar timber; at two o'clock P. M. we gained the top, the scene of the country became beautiful and level; passed through several groves of pine and cedar timber; at 11 o'clock we came to a stream affording an abundance of grass and timber, where we encamped, having come 14 miles.

Jesse Harritt

September 23, 1845
to A Spring 18 Beried 4 persons heare
Samuel Parker

Went about 12 miles, striking away from the river and camping upon a small branch of it. Had a long and hard pull in the morning to ascend the hill spoken of yesterday, but once up we felt amply repaid the trouble of climbing by the prospect which lay before us. There were the Cascade mountains stretching along the western horizon, apparently not more than forty miles distant, forming a dark outline, varied by an occasional snow-peak, which would rise lofty and spire-like, as if it were a monument to departed greatness.

James Field

Started late; had good road; traveled 12 miles; stopped at nine o'clock at a spring; found good grass; no wood except a little sage.

Jesse Harritt

September 24, 1845
traveled all day and that nite 25 all day and all that nite and struck water ABout 10 the 26 day 65 Many codent (get) to water and water was taken them 32 in number heare we beried 6 persons
Samuel Parker

Went about 15 miles, camping at a spring in the midst of the plains, without a single landmark to tell its situation.
James Field

James Field's journal ended with this entry. He contracted the fever that was killing other members of the migration, and he became too weak to continue writing.

Road good; traveled 14 miles through the level plain and stopped for the night without wood or water.
Jesse Harritt

The wagons traveled on:

September 25, 1845
Made an early start; traveled six miles and encamped on Chutes or Fall River. (About 11 miles NW of Madras.) This river is the most singular in character of any we have seen; it washes the eastern margin of the Cascade Mountains and flows with a rapid current through a deep cavern of rock, having a channel from 20 to 30 yards wide and is from 300 to 400 feet below the level plain.
Jesse Harritt

The main wagon train traveled north where they camped

175

for the night on the precipitous rim of the Crooked River Gorge. The next morning they followed the rim east, where, within sight of Smith Rocks, which they called "Bluffs of the Followers of Meek", they were able to cross the river. Near the present site of Madras, the two groups sighted each other and began traveling together once again. Nearly 200 wagons camped near Sagebrush Spring, about 1/2 mile east of Gateway, on September 26, 1845.

September 26, 1845
many codent get to water and water was taken to them 32 in number heare we beried 6 persons.
Samuel Parker

Turned a northeast direction; traveled three miles and encamped at a good spring in company with about 200 wagons. (Sagebrush Spring)
Jesse Harritt

Mt. Jefferson and Mt. Hood loom constantly to the west and northwest now. A baby born here, in sight of Mt. Jefferson, was named Jefferson Waymire. Two months later, Jefferson Waymire died. A year or two later, William Helm established his donation land claim in the Willamette Valley, within sight of the west side of Mt. Jefferson.

September 27, 1845
laid by heare my wife tuck sick and child missis Butts not expected to live
Samuel Parker

Laid by all day to rest.
Jesse Haritt

I looked near Gateway, for Sagebrush Spring, but did not find it. In Gateway I found an abandoned railway station and an old general merchandise store. The store had the look of a once prosperous place, but it was boarded up tight. A herd of seven fairly late-model American automobiles nuzzled the shady side of the old building and a young woman hung wash from lines behind the store.

From Sagebrush Spring the wagons traveled east through Lyle Gap, then turned north near present Willowdale to Shaniko Flats, then northwest toward The Dalles. I, too, headed for Lyle Gap and The Dalles.

September 28, 1845

went ten miles 10
Samuel Parker

Traveled eight miles and encamped on a small branch
Jesse Harritt

September 29,1845
all day giting up hill laid with out water beried 3 heare 3
Samuel Parker

This morning we ascended a huge mountain; were compelled to double our teams; gained the top at 12 o'clock we continued our journey over the level plain until eight o'clock, when we encamped on the margin of a bluff, down which we descended 200 feet and found a small stream of water (Bakeoven Creek) shaded by a beautiful grove of pine trees.
Jesse Harritt

When Meek reached the Deschutes River at Sherar's Bridge, about 6 miles north of Maupin, word came that Henry J. Noble, whose sons had died along the trail, was riding hard to catch him. Noble swore to kill Meek before sundown. Meek persuaded an Indian to carry one end of a rope across the Deschutes. The rope was secured to rocks on either side and Meek suspended himself from this rope by tying a rope beneath his arms and rigging a "running noose" to slide along the first rope. He was the first white man across the river. Nathan Olney followed, and then Meek's wife, Elizabeth. They had not been across the river long when two armed men rode up and asked where Meek was. Told that he had gone across the river, one of the men replied that it was just as well, because his own two sons were now buried. (from the diary of Samuel Hancock, in The Terrible Trail, p. 127.)

Meek rode into The Dalles that afternoon (September 29, 1845), bought pullies, ropes, food and other supplies to send back with a rescue party.

"He requested the missionaries for a guide to deliver the articles, but was refused. Resenting the extra labor put upon them by emigrants, these teachers and examples of Christian brotherhood let Meek know that they were appointed by the Mission Board to teach the Indians the word of the Lord, not to minister relief to the annual hoard of refugees from the states, nor did they run a guide service for those who became lost. They themselves were far too busy."[10]

September 30, 1845
travled all day and till in the nite and Came to water   35 Comeing in all nite 5 beried here
Samuel Parker

Traveled 10 miles and encamped on a small branch; found a few willows.
Jesse Harritt

Meek knew he couldn't safely return to the wagon train, so he persuaded an old friend, Major Moses "Black" Harris to take the horses and supplies to the immigrants at the river. Harris and two Indian assistants reached the river on September 30. Stephen and Elizabeth Meek and Nathan Olney went on to the Willamette Valley.

October 1, 1845

went 9
    Samuel Parker

Had bad road; traveled six miles and encamped at a good spring; found a few willows. (Near east side of Buck Hollow)
    Jesse Harritt

The immigrants traveled down Buck Hollow Creek to the mouth of Buck Hollow, about half a mile east of Sherar's Bridge. There they strung more ropes across the raging Deschutes and secured them to rocks on either side of the river. They removed the wheels from their wagons, caulked the wagon beds and drew the wagon beds, suspended from pullies attached to the ropes, across the river.

October 2, 1845

got to the deshutes river missis Butts dyed this day my wife and Child and second daughter all sick 9
    Samuel Parker

Road continues bad; traveled four miles and encamped on Chutes or Fall River.
    Jesse Harritt

Intense pain struck Mrs. Butts as her family's wagon,

traveling now behind Parker's wagon, began the descent to the Deschutes. The descent was so steep, that, once started, the wagon could not be stopped until the ground leveled out beneath it at the bottom of the hill. By the time the wagon arrived at the bottom of the hill, Samuel Parker's friend, Mrs. Butts, was dead.

October 3, 1845
crossed the deshutes river in a wagon body and tuck the wagons Apart and tuck A wheale at A time by ropes
this day my 2 small boys tuck sick gideon and george and susan my forth girl 6 of my family sick at one time
Samuel Parker

Spent the day in crossing the river. Had no timber to make boats; were compelled to make boats of our wagon beds to cross our families and goods.
Jesse Harritt

The immigrants traveled along the bottom of Buck Hollow Creek to the mouth of Buck Hollow, about half a mile east of Sherar's Bridge. There they strung more ropes across the Deschutes and secured them to rocks on either side of the river. They removed the wheels from their wagons, caulked the wagon beds and drew them, suspended from pullies attached to the ropes, across the river.

Warm Springs Indians still fish from platforms that cling to rocks above raging waters on the south side of the Deschutes, just west of Sherar's Bridge. Just west of the fishermen, above the falls, hundreds of river-runners pull their colorful craft to the north shore of the Deschutes every summer day. Buses, vans, and station wagons line the road on that side, retrieving the wet, weary, sunburned rafters and transporting them back upriver. In the interval of time between raft and van, rafters saunter down to watch the fishermen across the river. The fishermen sit on inverted buckets, long-handled fishnets in hand, and watch placidly as the parade of gaudily-attired recreationists passes. The river crashes between the groups like a border in time. Stephen Meek would still feel comfortable on the south bank.

October 4, 1845
Rigged our wagons, loaded up and traveled three miles to a delightful stream shaded by a few cottonwood trees where we encamped for the night.
Jesse Harritt

October 5, 1845
day I got all over and went 3 miles to A small Creek Heare we beried missis Butts and 3 more
Samuel Parker

Traveled 12 miles and encamped in a beautiful white oak grove (Tygh Ridge); found no water.
Jesse Harritt

Mrs. Butts lies on top of a knoll, a mile or two from the Deschutes, and about mile from where the wagons topped Tygh Ridge. Her grave is a couple of miles behind a locked gate, near a clutch of abandoned farm buildings. A few hardy juniper trees dot this rolling grassland, and the wind forever blows. I stood at her grave one July afternoon and tried to imagine the saddened little group of settlers burying her and three others, whose names have been forgotten, on this windswept hillside. The graves are far apart and heaped with rocks. Each might be mistaken for a pile made by a farmer intending to clear a field of rocks.

A couple of years ago, two markers were placed on Mrs.

Butts' grave. After more than 140 years of looking like just another pile of rocks, it was also surrounded by a fence made of round, treated lumber. The man who unlocked the gate for me told me that there'd been a sort of memorial service when the markers were placed. "Channel 2 even showed up," he said. I wondered what Mrs. Butts would think of that.

October 6, 1845
the wagons started on and I went Back for A horse and ox and Cow got the horse but never got the ox nor cow my family sow I codent Stay overtuck the wagons About midnight all my family verry bad 27
Samuel Parker

Made an early start; traveled five miles to a branch (Fifteenmile Creek or Pine Hollow); where we stopped to take breakfast, rested two hours and started again; five miles further brought us to another stream (Eightmile Creek) where we encamped for the night.
Jesse Harritt

The wagons topped Tygh Ridge east of Dufur, then dropped into a countdown of creeks: 15 Mile Creek, 8 Mile Creek, 5 Mile Creek, 3 Mile Creek and, finally, The Dalles.

October 7, 1845
this morning nothing to eat got to the mishion at dark 17 got in A house with my family got something to eat
this was the first day we had done without something to eat But some of the Company had been with out bread fore 15 days and had to live on pore beef with out any thing else
I will just say pen and tong will both fall short when they gow to tell the suffering the Company went through
Samuel Parker

Eight miles brought us to the mission (The Dalles) on the

Columbia River, where we got a fresh supply of provisions.
    Jesse Harritt

The Methodist Mission near The Dalles, was apparently more a bastion of capitalism than of Christian charity. H. D. Martin, in a letter appearing in the St. Joseph, Missouri, <u>Gazette</u>, on August 21, 1846, saw it like this: "We found the missionary, Mr. Waller, ready to devour the poor starved emigrant by charging exorbitant prices for everything and very unaccommodating in every way, and nothing without specie of cattle at one third of their value...."

Immigrants received only the supplies they could pay or trade for. Staples such as flour were sold to the immigrants at double the Willamette Valley price. Those without trade goods, money, or cattle to trade received nothing, and had to subsist on salmon or beets or by making broth from such things as salmon skins, bacon rinds and other discarded but edible items.

The Mission was, in fact, overrun with immigrants arriving daily in varying degrees of need to which it was ill-equipped to minister. The entire immigration consisted of 500 wagons and 2500 people. About 225 wagons and 1000 people followed Meek. Mountain fever combined with a scarcity of resources to make the Mission a gloomy place in the fall of 1845.

Those who were physically able made their way to the Willamette Valley as soon as they could. They now had to choose again between overland routes, one to the south and one to the north of Mount Hood, or drifting the Columbia on log rafts and large canoes. Because it was late in the year, most took to the river. Many left their cattle behind, planning to return for them in the spring. Those with enough money hired rafts and canoes and were quickly transported downriver. Others felled trees and built their own rafts. Still others settled in for the winter, planning to continue their journey in the spring.

Reverend Alvin F. Waller, who was in charge of the Mission at The Dalles, must have liked the idea of having a fellow Methodist minister around, because he welcomed William Helm and his family and persuaded them to spend the winter. Years later, his son, Richard Watson Helm talked with Fred Lockley:

At that time the only two buildings at The Dalles were two large log buildings. Mr. Waller lived in one, Mr. Brewer in the other. We moved into the Brewer house and spent the winter with them. Mr. Brewer was a good farmer, kind-hearted and easy to get along with. During the winter Father helped him with the work about the place and also assisted Mr. Waller in his work with the Indians.

One day about 150 Indians—Cayuse Indians and others—rode up to our place and surrounded Mr. Brewer's house. They were dressed in war paint and armed with a few flintlocks and with bows and arrows. They held a war dance. Father asked Mr. Brewer what it meant. He said the Indians had come from the upper country and he was afraid it meant trouble. Father said, "We can't remain in uncertainty. I'll go out and see what they mean.

The Indians were dancing, not exactly in a circle, but in the form of an elipse. Each warrior had a knife in his hand with which, as he danced, he would lunge savagely at a supposed enemy. Some of the Indians were beating a drum and the Indians who were dancing sang a queer monotonous chant. As they sang they would leap high into the air, their arms and hands flailing around like the sails of a windmill.

Father opened the door and stepped out. Mr. Brewer shut the door and put the bar up. As Father stepped out the chief of the war party gave a command and all but about a dozen Indians squatted down, while the others surrounded Father and continued their war dance around him.

I was just a little chap, but I can remember as though it were yesterday seeing my father surrounded by those half-naked, savage, leaping, yelling Indians. The chief was sitting cross-legged like a tailor. He sprang up as though his legs were wire springs and, coming up to my father, said, "What you doing here? You no 'fraid of the Indians?"

My father put out his hand and said, "How do you do?"

The chief was a fine-looking Indian. He held out his hand and said, "What you come here for?"

My father said, "I have come to find out what you are here for. Have you come to kill the men who came across the plains to tell you of the white man's god and to bring you His book? I can talk to you better in the house. Come on in with me—if you are not afraid."

The Indian said something to the other Indians and came with Father into the house.

Dinner was just about to be served, so Father invited the Indian to sit down with us at the table. Before eating we followed our usual custom, which was to kneel around the table while Father or one of the others asked a blessing. The Indian knelt and never moved a muscle till the prayer was over. He ate dinner, after which Father told him why the missionaries had come to Oregon.

Finally, he said, "You good man," and, going to the door, he called to the Indians and made a short talk to them. A moment later he mounted his horse and all of the Indians rode off at full speed.

I have always thought the Indians intended to kill us, for they were in a surly mood when they came, and it was only two years later that they rose and killed Dr. Marcus Whitman, his wife, and many others at the Whitman Mission.

The next April we put our two wagons and the family on a flatboat made of logs and started down the Columbia River. We landed above the Cascades, where they made a portage of the goods and turned the raft loose. The Indians caught it below the Cascades, and, after making some minor repairs in it, the goods were reloaded, the family got aboard, and we floated down the Columbia to the mouth of the Sandy, where the goods were landed, the wagons set up, and the oxen brought up and yoked and we drove to Oregon City. From there we drove up the valley where Father gave a settler a pony for his squatter's *right to 640 acres of land and his cabin.*11

For the next few years, William Helm "rode all over the country, preaching wherever a group of settlers got together..." His five sons cleared brush, cut fence rails, fenced and plowed, transforming that 640 acres of brush into a farm. He then sold the farm and took up a donation land claim 12 miles south of Salem, a mile north of where the Santiam River crosses Interstate 5.

*We boys worked on this farm, near Parrish's Gap, till it was said to be one of the finest farms in the entire neighborhood. My father felt that the Lord had called him to preach, so he stayed on the job, regardless of other distractions or attractions. My father sold his donation land claim to Mr. Looney, for $8000,which in those days was a big price.*12

Maybe it is appropriate that the northwest corner of this old preacher's donation land claim is today anchored by a decrepit old barn that for years bore the message, "SOLDIERS OF THE CROSS ARMOR UP!" Recently that message was obscured by someone with a bucket of white paint, but a new one, printed in block letters on the roof and visible from the southbound lane tells travelers, "IN JESUS NAME". A large dairy farm occupies most of the original land claim.

William and Martha Helm bought and sold several farms in Marion County and then, according to a letter written by Richard Watson Helm in 1865 to his sister Libbie, "Father very sagely concluded that farming is not his calling and bought half of Doc Smith's drug store and has put his hopeful son Coke in it to sell out the poisonous medicines to kill the poor, deluded folks of Salem and vicinity..."

Eventually they moved to Portland where, in January, 1890, they died within three weeks of one another. He was 89, she was 81. They were married for 65 years. They lie in an unmarked grave in Portland's Riverside Cemetery.

Jesse Harritt became the Reverend Jesse Harritt and spent his later years preaching the gospel in Willamette Valley settlements. He took up a donation land claim in Marion County, where, to make it easy on his parishioners, he raised his own food. He died on his farm on March 27, 1888. He was 80 years old.

Within a week of their arrival at the Mission, Mrs. Parker gave birth to a son, James Luther Samuel Parker. Weakened by the rigors of the Terrible Trail, Mrs. Parker and the child soon died. Before Samuel Parker and his other children left the Mission, his daughter, Virginia, also died.

Of their arrival in The Dalles, Samuel Parker later wrote:

thare my wife and Child died and I staid till the 3 of November when I left fore oregon City in A large Canoe with four indiens for which I give sixty dollars

when I started the wet wether had set in I did not expect to git to the City with my fore sick Children and my oldes girl that was sick I was looking all the time fore hir to die I tuck my seete in the Canoe by hir and held hir up and the same at nite when I Come to the Cascade falls I had to make A portige of 3 miles I put my sick girl in A blanket and pack hir and onely rested once that day we maid the portige with the help of my fore indiens and my oldest boy and oldest girl boath had never been sick one minet on the Road

on the 8 I landed at oregon City wet hungry and all most wore out with my family most all sick the youngest sone got well but it was 19 days after I landed till my oldest stood alone harty and well now

frome winchester Vanburen County	
to St. Joy on the missory River	*247*
frome Saint Jow	
to fort lareny on plat river	*560*
frome fort laremy to fort Bridger	*382*
from fort Bridger to fort Hall	*230*

frome fort Hall to fort Boisy 282
frome fort Boisy to the Dals or mishion 509
to oregon City <u>120</u>
  2330

total frome missory River to oregon City 2083
  Samuel Parker

Samuel Parker served as postmaster for Salem in 1853 and later served several terms in the state legislature. He took up a donation land claim just south of Salem, on land now occupied by the Oregon State Penitentiary. He died in 1888, at the age of 89.

James Field's last journal entry was September 24, when he became too ill to write. From that date he was carried, dragged, or, occasionally, crawled to the Mission at The Dalles and then to the Willamette Valley. He recovered from mountain fever and settled for a few years in Portland.

News of the Whitman Massacre in 1847 panicked the residents of Portland, who believed that they were about to be attacked by Indians. In February, 1848, Field, now fully recovered, volunteered to ride to San Francisco with a dispatch requesting that a ship with arms and ammunition be sent to Portland immediately. He and 15 other volunteers made it through the Willamette Valley with ease, but deep snow in the mountains kept them from proceeding any further. "For some reason the expected attack from the Indians was averted, and Portland was not destroyed," according to the <u>Port Chester</u> (New York) <u>Daily Record</u> of May 11, 1903.

In 1849, he left Oregon for Missouri, a 2000 mile trip, on horseback. To avoid Indian trouble on the Oregon Trail he traveled south through the Willamette Valley and Rogue River Valley. Along the way, they met a group from Sutter's Fort, who failed to mention the gold strike, so they traveled on. By the time they arrived in the east, the entire country knew about the gold strike. Field went straight back to San Francisco to prospect for gold. A year or so later he returned to Portland, where he lived for many years.

In 1879, in answer to an inquiry prompted by the publication of the portions of his journal in the <u>Willamette Farmer</u>, published in Portland, Oregon, between April 18, 1879 and August 1, 1879,Field wrote:

> *Port Chester, N. Y.*
> *June 3, 1879*

Friend Clarke:

Through the kindness of my old friend, R. Weeks, of Portland, I am in receipt of three numbers of your paper, containing installments of my diary kept while crossing the plains in '45, with a request that I may complete it from memory. This it is impossible for me to do, as it was cut short by my illness with camp fever, which destroyed all memory of what transpired during the remainder of the journey.

I have an indistinct recollection of crossing the Deschutes river in a wagon body caulked tight, and drawn back and forth by ropes, of being carried and laid upon a bed among the rocks that lined the riverbanks where we crossed, and of arriving at The Dalles so helpless that it was necessary to lift me out of and into the wagon like a baby. Then I remember going down to the Cascades in a boat such as the Hudson Bay Co. then used on the river, of walking and crawling past the first steep rapid, then getting into a canoe with some Indians and running the remainder of the rapids to the landing place of the old Callapooia, Capt. Cook owner and master; then of sailing down the Columbia and up the Willamette to Linton, a place on the west bank of the river below Portland, and then having the only wagon-road to the Tualatin plains below Oregon City from the river.

From Linton to Oregon City I was a fellow-passenger with old Mr. Fleming, the pioneer printer, so long connected with the press at that place, and I think it was late in November when we arrived there.

When I returned here overland in the spring of '48 I deposited the diary with Capt. H. B. Riggs, of Polk county, and when I returned to Oregon in '50, finding that he had used the blank leaves in the book to keep his business accounts on, I left it with him. If it is still my property,—and I know of no reason why it should not be,—please hand it to the Society of Pioneers, of Oregon. With my compliments I herewith present it to them.

It was written up daily after all my other duties as teamster and general assistant about the camp were performed. It has never been revised by me, and I hope my old companions will overlook any errors I have made. Your friend,

James Field

James Field died in May, 1903, in Port Chester, New York, not far from where he was born. He was 80 years old.

For Stephen Meek, the 1845 immigration was just another day at the office. In his autobiography it rates just four sentences:

In March, 1845, I went to New Orleans and then up the river to St. Louis, where I got letters of recommendation from Fitzpatrick, Wm. Sublette and Rob. Campbell, which secured me the position as guide to the immense emigrant train of 480 wagons then preparing to go to Oregon. We started on the 11th of May, 1845, on which day I first saw Elizabeth Schoonover, whom I married a week later.

"Arriving at Fort Hall, one third of the train under Wm. B. Ide, of bear flag notoriety, went to California, guided by the old trapper, Greenwood. The remainder, I conducted safely to Oregon, the first large train of wagons ever taken there.[13]

F. T. Humphrey, in an article published in 1938, calls Meek Oregon's Hard Luck Pioneer. "Consider," he asks us, "his fortuitous fate:

First, his outstanding career was overshadowed by that of his flashier, more robust brother, Joe Meek, whose exploits, such as his hanging of the five Whitman massacre Indians at Oregon City, made history.

Second, he was blamed in large measure for the disastrous immigration of 1845 and Meek's hunch that he could find a short-cut into the heart of the Willamette Valley from Fort Boise, thus saving 200 miles of weary travel, was later fully justified.

Third, he made a fortune gold mining in California, invested it in a valuable land grant in what is now the rich Watsonville, California, district, and then lost it all ($50,000) when a court ruled that the aged man from whom he bought it was mentally incompetent.

Fourth, John A. Sutter, founder of Fort Sutter and personal friend of Meek's, once offered Meek 10 acres near his embarcadero on the Sacramento River for an English shotgun Meek owned. Meek laughed at Sutter, but that 10 acres is now the heart of Sacramento.

Fifth, Meek and others of the great immigration train of 1845 discovered by accident what was later called the Blue Bucket Mine (on the Malheur River), as they trekked through the Cascades in Oregon, dipping gold nuggets from the stream in a blue bucket, yet the "mine" could never be found again..."[14]

Stephen and Elizabeth Meek settled near Oregon City, but when the rumor of gold in California spread to Oregon in 1848, they headed south. For short periods during the next 15 years, Meek owned butcher shops in Coloma and Santa Cruz, California but his main occupation during that time was mining.

When Elizabeth died in 1865, he began again to drift wherever the winds of opportunity blew. He guided freight trains and hunting parties, prospected for the Blue Bucket Mine, and worked as wagon master, scout, and Indian fighter for the U. S. Government.

Meek had spent the winter of 1833 on the shore of Tulare Lake, in northern California. He was the first white man in that area and, after a lifetime of adventure in other places, he returned to what had, by then, become Siskiyou County: "Being now advanced in years and having lost all the money my good fortune and hard labor had brought me, I was compelled to take to the mountains to secure a livelihood. I went to Red Bluff, bought animals and traps and have ever since been trapping the waters of Sacramento, Pit, McLeod, Scott, Trinity and other rivers of northern California."

Stephen Meek died in Scott Valley, California, in January, 1889. He was 83. In its January 19, 1889 issue, the The <u>Scott Valley News</u> expressed "... universal regret at his death and (it) does no more than justice to the memory of the first white man who came to Siskiyou County in saying that he was a type of the true pioneer—an honest man."

"About all that could be added," said F. T. Humphrey in the <u>Oregon Journal</u> in 1938, "is that Stephen H. L. Meek had what it takes to pioneer in a new land. He positively refused to let hardship and bad luck get him down."

In July, 1990, over a span of five years, I had finally traveled the Terrible Trail, or as close as I could get without cutting fences or driving over crops, all the way from the Idaho border to The Dalles. The experience left me full of admiration for the 200 families who risked all on an untried route to new lives in Oregon. Until I traveled it myself, I did not appreciate the immensity of their achievement nor the vast and hostile nature of the land they chose to cross. It is a long, hard trip from Nyssa to The Dalles, even today, traveling in a Jeep, mostly on roads.

For Stephen Meek, also, I feel admiration. Though the immigrants threatened his life again and again, he would not abandon them in the desert. "I have brought you here, and will take you off, if you will go," he said, and he did.

There is a sense of timelessness in the desert, a feeling that Stephen Meek and Samuel Parker might have walked there yesterday. In its wildest places, they would see little changed, but the size and number of those wild places is continually diminished by the mad rush of industry. White plastic claim-stakes sprout everywhere today, reminders of the desert's threatened status. The strip-miners are coming and they mean to have the desert just as surely as the clearcutters took our forests.

As I reread these pages, I am reminded of sore feet, thirst, exhaustion, loneliness, mosquitoes, heat, nasty little flies. I see again some of the preposterous ideas I once had--that I could carry a 70-pound pack across 200 desert miles in the middle of summer, for example.

Especially, though, I am reminded of the great gifts to be found in the desert. There I found stillness, peace, stark beauty, a place for contemplation and inspiration. The desert is a great humbler, a fine teacher, a refuge from the hurly-burly of our industrial society.

You can still hear Old Man Coyote's crazy song almost every night along the Terrible Trail, borne along on the wonderful, sage-scented desert wind. Sam Parker and Stephen Meek and the others still walk there as well, and sometimes, through the heat or in the moonlight, you will see them, plodding ever westward: *"tuck what is caled the meeks Cut of misses Butts tuck Sick this day..."*

On the Necessity
of
Monkeywrenching

Any fool can destroy trees. They cannot run away; and if they could, they would still be destroyed—chased and hunted down as long as fun or a dollar could be got out of their bark hides, branching horns, or magnificent bole backbones.

Few that fell trees plant them; nor would planting avail much towards getting back anything like the noble primeval forests. During a man's life only saplings can be grown, in the place of old trees—tens of centuries old—that have been destroyed. It took more than three thousand years to make some of the trees in these western woods—trees that are still standing in perfect strength and beauty, waving and singing in the mighty forest...

Through all the wonderful, eventful centuries...God has cared for these trees, saved them from drought, disease, avalanches, and a thousand straining leveling tempests and floods; but he cannot save them from fools—only Uncle Sam can do that.[1]

John Muir

I began with the intention of writing a book about the wonder of Oregon's wild places, where, at certain magic times, it is possible to be simultaneously in touch with the present and the mythical and historical past. This endeavor took me to wild places all over our state, where, frequently, after viewing the heavy-handed treatment of a fragile natural place by those who had found a way to squeeze a dollar out of it, a feeling of rage replaced that of wonder.

Typical of such a time was the night a couple of years ago when I lay down to sleep in a clearcut in southern Oregon. It was late and I was very tired. I threw my sleeping bag on a spot made flat some muddy day months before by the spinning of a Caterpillar tractor. The ground around was scraped and churned, the work of tractors and skidders and loaders. Plastic oil bottles, rusty cable, and mouldering debris from old lunches lay about the site. I was disgusted but too tired to move on, so I spent that night in a graveyard of stumps that straddled the Pacific Crest National Scenic Trail for nearly a mile.

A nation of men and women made cowards by our possessions, we stand politely by while our streams and rivers are dammed, damned, and polluted, our forests hacked down, our desert cratered and poisoned, and our lush prairies stripped bare of their native grasses. We pony up tax money to subsidize those who degrade our environment, reclaiming ruined grassland for those whose cattle overgraze the public range, building roads for timberbeasts to clearcut and truck away our national forests, giving away the desert to anyone who can scrape, gouge or blast a few dollars from its delicate surface.

Most of those who actively oppose the tide of industrial destruction that is sweeping away our wild places indulge themselves in benign activities. They carry placards on Earth Day, write to politicians and newspapers and send money to environmental organizations. But among the things I've learned in the past few years is this: one who endeavors to preserve our wild places by writing polite letters to congressmen and senators and sending money to mainstream environmental organizations may as well expect to cause a flood by pissing in the Columbia River. Congress will only act to save what's left after the last dollar of profit has been wrung from our federal lands by those who own the lawmakers.

Sometime in the not-too-distant future, most of us will shrug and wring our hands in gestures of helpless resignation

196

as we try to explain to our children that we tried, but were unable to save the land from those who ruined it. We will talk about demonstrations, letters, the Sierra Club and the Oregon Natural Resources Council, legislation that was introduced and then gutted by special interests before becoming law, and we'll damn the lumbermen, miners, stockmen and others who manipulated public opinion, bought our lawmakers, took our wild places and converted them to dollars. We will wake up one morning and it will all be gone, and we will sigh and say we tried, but could not save it. We will have trouble, as we tell this story, meeting the eyes of our children.

Others (Environmental guerrillas. Dave Foreman and Edwrd Abbey call them monkeywrenchers.) will confront the industrial beast more directly. Not that we can stop it in its tracks, because we cannot. It is too big, too powerful, greased with too much money, owns too many politicians. But a few monkeywrenchers can slow it, maybe slow it enough so that when our lawmakers finally take meaningful action on behalf of the environment, something somewhere will be left to save.

Dave Foreman's 1985 book, <u>Ecodefense, A Field Guide to Monkeywrenching</u>, is a catalogue of destructive acts complete with diagrams and instructions for everything from spiking trees to taking down billboards to disabling heavy equipment. The book and its violent acts against machinery and tools seemed extreme to me when it was published. The environmental destruction I have seen in Oregon in the past four years and the bias of Oregon's politicians toward their corporate benefactors has changed my view. Now it is clear to me that by far the most destructive and radical acts are those committed against Nature by timber companies and cyanide heap leach miners. The torching of a tractor or the spiking of a few trees pale to insignificance when compared to the violence wreaked on the environment by a single clearcut.

"It is time," Foreman tells us, "for women and men,

individually and in small groups, to act heroically and admittedly illegally in defense of the wild, to put a monkeywrench into the gears of the machine destroying natural diversity. This strategic monkeywrenching can be safe, it can be easy, it can be fun, and—most importantly—it can be effective in stopping timber cutting, road building, overgrazing, oil and gas exploration, mining, dam building, powerline construction, off-road-vehicle use, trapping, ski area development and other forms of destruction of the wilderness, as well as cancerous suburban sprawl."[2]

Indeed, it is time to protect Oregon's wild places. It is past time. The industrial beast aims to take it all, every wild place. If there is a dollar to be gained there is nowhere safe from bulldozer, chainsaw, dump truck and cow. Proof of this is everywhere apparent to those awake enough to perceive it.

It is well known that Henry David Thoreau once spent a night in the Concord, Massachusetts jail. He refused to pay his poll tax in protest of the U. S. government's support of slavery.

When his friend, Ralph Waldo Emerson, visited him in jail, he asked, "Why, Henry, what are you doing in there?"

Thoreau replied, "Why, Waldo, what are you doing out there?" He understood that not resisting is tacitly supporting. "Under a government which imprisons any unjustly," he said, "the true place for a just man is also a prison."

If Thoreau returns from wherever he has gone to witness our tacit support of the rape of our environment by the industrial beast, he will ask us, each and every one of us, "What are you doing out there?"

The timber industry has already converted more than 90% of Oregon's ancient forests to stumps and two-by-fours, yet it daily bellows like a wounded dinosaur for more, more, more. Corporate thugs spew fear and hatred for conservation and conservationists in hundreds of small towns in the Pacific Northwest, blaming the spotted owl and "preservationists" for job losses, all the while ignoring the real culprits: overcutting, log exports, sawmill technology.

As I write, Oregon sawmills are glutted with old growth logs from our national forests because of Mark Hatfield's "Rider from Hell", the infamous timber "compromise" of 1989. Senator Hatfield duped Congress into mandating that an area equal to a strip three-quarters of a mile wide stretching from the Columbia River to the California border be clearcut to feed the ravenous appetite of the timber industry. This is a clearcut big enough to see from the moon. In the past week, while timber industry executives demanded that Oregon's wilderness area boundaries be redrawn to free up more trees for their sawmills, Senator Bob Packwood said he would work to exempt the spotted owl from the Endangered Species Act, thereby sending even more of Oregon's ancient forest to the sawmill.

Have no doubt, the timber industry wants it all—every tree, every wild place. The lumber barons own our senators and have the money to buy all the other politicians and television advertising they need to facilitate the clearcutting of our forests. As long as a tree stands in Oregon, the timberbeast will be there, chainsaw at the ready.

So, when you go out in the woods today, take along a few 60 penny spikes and a three-pound hammer. Spike a few trees, scatter some nails along a logging road, remove ribbons and other markings from trees, throw a monkeywrench into the gears of the timberbeast.

Industrial demolition doesn't stop at the forest boundary. The horde of white claimstakes spreading across the Oregon Desert spells trouble for this most wild and delicate area. Read about strip mining in Appalachia and Montana and about cyanide heap leaching in Nevada and in Baker County and you will have an idea of what is coming our way. As long as there is a dollar's worth of gold, someone with a bulldozer will be there to gouge, scrape and poison the desert in search of it.

So, spring to the defense of the desert. Simple activities like pulling up survey stakes and tossing them away or flattening truck tires annoy the industrial beast and raise the price of doing business. More costly to the industrial beast but more risky to the monkeywrencher are the demolition or disabling of bulldozers or earth-movers. Each time the price of defoliating the desert goes up—each time a site must be resurveyed, or a tire or a tractor replaced—the profit margin shrinks. If the profit goes away, so does the strip mining project. You <u>can</u> save the desert.

"If a stranger batters your door down with an axe, threatens your family and yourself with deadly weapons, and proceeds to loot your home of whatever he wants," Edward Abbey reminds us, "he is committing what is universally recognized—by law and morality—as a crime. In such a situation the householder has both the right and the obligation to defend himself, his family, and his property by whatever means necessary...The American wilderness, what little remains, is now undergoing exactly such an assault."[3]

Abbey's metaphorical stranger, the industrial beast, has battered down Oregon's door, looted our home of much that he wants. Now he aims to take it all, to subject every wild place to the bulldozer and chainsaw. It is the right and the obligation of everyone who loves Oregon, loves her wild places, to defend her.

Indeed, it is time. What are you doing out there?

Epilogue

You might think, in the face of all the tools and the quick and clever ways we use them to demolish our environment, that Coyote, that old trickster, would give up, slink off into the night, never to be seen or heard from again. It's true that he's a little more distant these days, harder to see over the clearcuts and claimstakes and the placid, oily lakes where our wild rivers used to be, but though I never quite tracked him down, I was close often enough to sense his presence. He's still out there, biding his time.

Early in their partnership, when Coyote, Lizard, and Bat caught salmon at the mouth of the Columbia, they learned that if they took more than they needed the salmon would be ashamed and not enter the river. The giant beaver, Wishpoosh; the sisters who hoarded all the fish; Wawa, the giant mosquito—suffered for greed, arrogance and selfishness, for forgetting the welfare of all the other folks who share our globe. Coyote works slowly, but the lesson is clear. I believe he'll get around to punishing the polluters, the stripminers, the clearcutters, the dam builders. Acid rain, global warming, holes in the ozone—who is to say these aren't more tricks, the old trickster doing his stuff on a cosmic scale? To paraphrase a bumper sticker:

COYOTE'S COMING
and he's pissed!

So, what to do until he arrives? Defend, of course. But, perhaps even more important, enjoy. Get out of your car. Walk on the earth. Visit wild places. Sleep beneath the stars. Sit on a rock while the early morning sun warms your bones. Breathe deep the fresh, wild wind. Feel the salty surf spray on your face, the gentle rain in your hair. Sip clear, sweet water from a mountain spring. Pick a sprig of juniper, roll it between your hands and savor its lovely, clean smell. Drowse an hour in a desert hot spring, Coyote's own spa. Hike to a mountain meadow. Climb a mountain. Run a wild river. Watch wildlife. Delight in wildness, for, as Henry Thoreau reminded us long ago, "In wildness is the preservation of the earth." In wildness is the preservation of us all.

Mike Helm
Eugene, Oregon
September 8, 1990

Notes

Frontispiece
Kinsella, W. P., "Frank Pierce, Iowa", <u>The Further Adventures of Slugger McBatt</u>, Houghton Mifflin, Co., 1988, p. 71.

In the Beginning
[1]Clark, Ella E. "George Gibbs' Account of Indian Mythology in Oregon and Washington Territories," <u>Oregon Historical Quarterly</u>, December, 1955, p. 299.

The Northwest Corner
[1]Kuykendall, G. B. "Origin of the Tribes." <u>History of the Pacific Northwest: Oregon and Washington, Volume II</u>, p. 62. North Pacific History Company, Portland, Oregon, 1889.

[2]Gill, John. "Superstitions and Ceremonies of Indians of Old Oregon", <u>Oregon Historical Quarterly</u>, XXIX, #4, December, 1928, p. 317.

[3]Curtis, Edward S. <u>The North American Indian</u>, Volume 8, 1911, p. 107.

[4]Ibid.

[5]Gill, p. 317-318.

[6]Lyman, H. S. "Indian Legends, and How I Came By Them". <u>Oregon Teachers Monthly</u>. February, 1904, pp. 28-31.

[7]Kalama, Lillie, "The Battle of the Winds". <u>Oregon Teachers Monthly</u>, January, 1904. (Hoolee was the southwind (the Chinook), Utyah the northwind.)

[8]Gill, p. 316.

April in the Desert
[1]Oregon Oddities, compiled by Oregon Writers' Project and Historical Records Survey, Work Projects Administration of Oregon, Portland, Oregon, undated

[2]Ramsey, Jarold, ed. <u>Coyote Was Going There</u>, University of Washington Press, Seattle, 1977, p. 232.

[3]Kuykendall, G. B. "Speelyai Fights Eenumtla," <u>History of The Pacific Northwest: Oregon and Washington</u>. North Pacific History Company, Portland, Oregon, 1889, p. 67.

[4]Byrd, Julian, "Byrd Relates Legend of Malheur Cave," <u>Burns Times-Herald</u>, Burns, Oregon, June 12, 1958.

Sky Lakes Wilderness
[1]Lockley, Fred. "Vittwia St. Clair Chapman Mickelson," <u>Conversations with Pioneer Women</u>. Rainy Day Press, Eugene, Oregon, 1981, pages 15-24.

[2] Crane, Warren E., <u>Totem Tales</u>. Fleming H. Revell Company, New York, 1932.

[3]Kuykendall, G. B. "Wawa, the Mosquito God," <u>History of the Pacific Northwest: Oregon and Washington, Volume II</u>. North Pacific History Company, Portland, Oregon, 1889, pages 74-75.

[4]<u>Oregon Oddities</u>, Compiled by the Oregon Writers' Project and Historical Records Survey of the Work Projects Administration of Oregon, Portland, undated.

[5]Clark, Ella. "George Gibbs' Account of Indian Mythology in Oregon and Washington Territories," Oregon Historical Quarterly, Volume 56, December, 1955. p. 302.

[6]Hillman, J. W., "The Discovery of Crater Lake", Steel Points, January, 1907, p. 78-79.

[7]Applegate, Oliver Cromwell, "The Indian Legend of Crater Lake", from a letter dated September 24, 1882, in a scrapbook in the Oregon Collection, University of Oregon Library. In an interesting paragraph in the same letter, Applegate tells Robert Miller, "I have been feeling too forlorn to write sensibly. I have allowed my sympathies for poor old Spokan Oke to make a little goose of me. I really cryed when the poor old fellow rode off, on his coffin. You are kind and can imagine how sorry I was for him. He was hanged last Friday and I have not been able to keep him out of my mind since. I visited him quite often in his cell and naturally grew Sympathetic."

Along the Terrible Trail
[1]Strycker, Lisa, "Cyanide mines worry conservationists", The Register Guard, Eugene, October 8, 1989, p. 8A.

[2]Robertson, Lance, "Coburg Hills old growth to be cut", The Register Guard, Eugene, Oregon, February 21, 1990, p. 3C.

[3]Strycker, 8A

[4]Wocjik, Donna, The Brazen Overlanders of 1845, Copyright by Donna Wojcik, 1976, p. 245.

[5]Bennett, Lucy Hall, in Souvenier of Western Women, edited by Mary Osborn Douthit, Portland, Oregon, 1905·

[6]John Herren's Diary for September 3, 1845 and Brother Mack,

the Frontier Preacher, printer T. G. Robinson, Portland, Oregon August 1, 1924. Citation from The Terrible Trail.

[7] Humphrey, F. T. "Oregon's Hard Luck Pioneer", Oregon Journal, January 16, 1938.

[9]Susannah Peterson, interviewed by Fred Lockley. In the Oregon Journal, no date.

[10]Wocjik, P. 308.

[11] Lockley, Fred. Conversations With Bullwhackers, Muleskinners, Etc. p. 139-40.

[12]Lockley, p. 140.

[13]Meek, Stephen Hall, The Autobiography of a Mountain Man. Pasadena, California: Glen Dawson, 1948. (First published as "A Sketch of Life of the First Pioneer", in *The Golden Era*, April, 1885 p. 9)

[14]Humphrey, F. T. "Oregon's Hard Luck Pioneer". Oregon Journal, Sunday, January 16, 1938.

On the Necessity of Monkeywrenching
[1]John Muir, quoted in Vickery, Jim dale, Wilderness Visionaries, ICS Books, Merrillville, Indiana, 1986, p. 89.

[2] Dave Foreman and Bill Haywood, Ecodefense: A Field Guide to Monkeywrenching, Second Edition, p. 14.

[3]Foreman and Haywood, p. 7.

List of Works Consulted

Adamson, Thelma. Folk Tales of the Coast Salish. New York: The American Folklore Society, 1934.

Allen, Ruth. "Jump-off-Joe". Oregon Teachers Monthly. May, 1905, p. 8-9.

Alt, David D. and Donald W. Hyndman. Roadside Geology of Oregon. Missoula, Montana: Mountain Press Publishing Company, 1978.

Anonymous. "The Chief's Shadow on Mt. Hood" The Pacific Monthly, Volume III, #4, February , 1900.

Anonymous. "Legend of Wallowa Lake Tells of Monster Swallowing Indians". Wallowa County Chieftain. Enterprise, Oregon July 30, 1959.

Anonymous. "Mountain Lore". Oregon Native Son. May, 1899.

Anonymous. "Shipwreck Survivors Remembered in Legends". Polk County Itemizer-Observer. Dallas, Oregon, March 17, 1976.

Applegate, O. C. "The Indian Legend of Crater Lake". from his scrapbook, Oregon Collection, University of Oregon Library.

Applegate, O. C. "The Klamath Legend of La-o". Steel Points, Volume I, #2, January, 1907. Pp. 75-76.

Bancroft, Hubert Howe. The Works of Hubert Howe Bancroft, Volume III: The Native Races, Myths, and Languages. San Francisco: A. L. Bancroft &

Company, 1883.

Bagley, Clarence B. Indian Myths of the Northwest. Seattle: Lowman & Hanford Company, 1930.

Beal, Merrill D. "I Will Fight No More Forever", Chief Joseph and the Nez Perce War. Seattle: University of Washington Press, 1977.

Bird, Annie Laurie. Old Fort Boise. Caldwell, Idaho: The Caxton Printers, 1971.

Boas, Franz. Kutenai Tales. Smithsonian Institution, Bureau of American Ethnology, #59. Washington: Government Printing Office, 1918.

Bowers, Fidelia March. An Account of the Wagon Train Mastered by Solomon Tetherow, including The Organizational Journal of An Emigrant Train of 1845 Captained by Solomon Tetherow. Eugene, Oregon: Lane County Historical Society, 1960.

Bright, Verne. "The Bridge of the Gods". Oregon Teachers Monthly, September, 1915, p. 2-3.

Brogan, Phil F. East of the Cascades. Portland, Oregon: Binfords & Mort, 1965.

Brogan, Joseph L. "Fight Between Coyote and Beaver Ends in Creating Columbia, Indian Legend Says". Portland: The Sunday Oregonian, March 22, 1931.

Bunnell, Clarence Orvel. Legends of the Klickitats: A Klickitat Version of the Story of the Bridge of the Gods. Portland: Metropolitan Press, 1933.

Clark, Keith and Lowell Tiller. Terrible Trail: the Meek Cutoff, 1845. Caldwell, Idaho: The Caxton Printers, 1966.

Clarke, Ella E. "The Bridge of the Gods in Fact and Fancy". Oregon Historical Society Quarterly, Volume #53, September, 1953, pp. 29-38.

Clarke, Ella E. "George Gibbs' Account of Indian Mythology in Oregon and

Washington Territories." <u>Oregon Historical Society Quarterly</u>, Volume #56, 1955, pp. 293-325.

Clarke, Ella E. "The Mythology of the Indians in the Pacific Northwest". <u>Oregon Historical Society Quarterly</u>, Volume 54, September, 1953, pp. 163-189.

Clarke, Ella E. "Some Nez Perce Traditions Told by Chief Armstrong". <u>Oregon Historical Society Quarterly</u>, September, 1952, pages 181-191.

Clarke, Samuel A. "Legend of the Cascades". <u>Harpers New Monthly Magazine</u>, February, 1874, pp. 313-319.

Clarke, Samuel A. "Legend of Nehalem". <u>Oregon Native Son</u>, Volume II, #1. May, 1900, pp. 35-40.

Clarke, Samuel A. <u>Pioneer Days of Oregon History, Volume I</u>. Portland: J. K. Gill Company, Portland, 1905.

Clarke, Samuel A. "Wrecked Beeswax and Buried Treasure". <u>Oregon Native Son</u>, Volume I, #5, September 1899, pp. 245-249.

Coffer, William E. <u>Spirits of the Sacred Mountains: Creation Stories of the American Indian</u>. New York: Van Nostrand Reinhold Company, 1978.

Colvig, William M. "The Legend of the White Deer", from his papers, Oregon Collection, University of Oregon Library.

Crane, Warren E. <u>Totem Tales</u>. New York: Fleming H. Revell Co. 1932.

Cressman, L. S. <u>The Sandal and the Cave: The Indians of Oregon</u>. Portland: Beaver Books, 1962.

Cummings, Sarah J. <u>Autobiography and Reminiscences of Sarah J. Cummings, Touchet, Washington</u>. La Grande, Oregon: La Grande Printing Company, 1908.

Curtin, Jeremiah. <u>Myths of the Modocs: Indian Legends of the Northwest</u>. New York: Benjamin Blom, Inc. 1971.

Curtis, Edward S. The North American Indian, Volumes 7, 8, & 9. Published by Edward S. Curtis, 1911.

Danvers, Clarence. "The Legend of the Lake". The Pacific Monthly, Volume III, #4. February, 1900.

Eells, M. undated letter to Post-Intelligencer.

El Hult, Ruby. Lost Mines and Treasures of the Pacific Northwest. Portland, Oregon: Binfords & Mort, 1974.

Evans, Samuel M. "The Breath of Chinook..." from an unknown magazine.

Ferguson, Denzel and Nancy. Oregon's Great Basin Country. Burns, Oregon: Gail Graphics, 1978.

Ferguson, Denzel and Nancy. Sacred Cows at the Public Trough. Bend, Oregon: Maverick Publications, 1983.

Fletcher, Colin. The New Complete Walker. New York: Alfred A. Knopf, 1977.

Foreman, Dave and Bill Haywood. Ecodefense: A Field Guide to Monkeywrenching, second edition. Tucson, Arizona: Ned Ludd, 1987.

Franzwa, Gregory M. The Oregon Trail Revisited. Patrice Press, Inc.

Gaston, Joseph. The Centennial History of Oregon, 1811-1912, Volume I. Chicago: S. J. Clark Publishing Co., 1912.

Gibbs, James A. Shipwrecks of the Pacific Coast, Portland, Oregon: Binford & Mort, Publishers, 1957.

Glassley, Ray H. Visit the Pacific Northwest. Portland, Binford & Mort, 1948, pages 147-149.

Hancock, Samuel. The Narrative of Samuel Hancock, 1845-1860. New York: Robert M. McBride, 1927.

Hart, John. Walking Softly in the Wilderness. San Francisco: Sierra Club Books, 1984.

Hawthorne, Julian, ed. History of Washington... Volume I. New York City: American Historical Publishing Company, 1893.

Hayward, Martha C. "The Legend of the Columbia". The Pacific Monthly, Volume IV, May-October, 1900.

Higgins, L. T. "Jump-off Joe". The Pacific Monthly, Volume VI. June-December, 1901.

Higgins, L. T. "Jump-off Joe". The Pacific Monthly, Volume X. July-December, 1903.

Hillman, J. W., "Discovery of Crater Lake". Steel Points, Volume I, #2, January, 1907. Pp. 77-79.

Hines, Donald M. Tales of the Nez Perce. Fairfield, Washington: Ye Galleon Press, 1984.

History of the Pacific Northwest, compiled and published by the North Pacific History Company of Portland, Oregon, 1889.

Horner, John B. Days and Deeds in the Oregon Country. Portland: J. K. Gill Company, 1928.

Horner, John B. "The Legend of Chin-Tim-I-Ni: How Chin-Tim-I-ni Came to Be The Ancient Name of Mary's Peak" Oregon Native Son, Volume II, #1. May, 1900. pp. 66-68.

Horner, John B. Oregon History and Early Literature: A Pictorial Narrative of the Pacific Northwest. Portland: J. K. Gill Co., 1931.

Humphrey, F. T. "Oregon's Hard Luck Pioneer" Oregon Journal, January 16, 1938.

John, Mae Peters (as told to Will Roddy) "Legend of Warm Springs".

Oregon Journal, Portland, March 28, 1958.

Judson, Katharine Berry. Myths and Legends of the Pacific Northwest, especially of Washington and Oregon. Chicago: A. C. McClurg & Co., 1910.

Kalama, Lillie. "The Battle of the Winds". Oregon Teachers Monthly, January, 1904, pp. 18-20.

Kane, Paul. Wanderings of an Artist Among the Indians of North America. Austin, Texas, and London: University of Texas Press.

Kerr, Mark Brickell. "Wimawita—A Legend of Crater Lake". The Pacific Monthly, Volume VI, June-December, 1901.

Kronenberg, O. K. "The Legend of Face Rock". The Oregon Motorist, Volume X, #12. September, 1930, p. 9+.

Kuykendall, G. B. History of the Pacific Northwest: Oregon and Washington, Volume II. Portland: North Pacific History Company, 1889.

Lamb, F. M. "The Spanish Castaways". Oregon Teachers Monthly, August, 1905, pp. 1-5.

Lapham, Stanton C. The Enchanted Lake: Mount Mazama and Crater Lake in Story, History, and Legend. Portland: J. K. Gill Company, 1931.

Lockley, Fred. Captain Sol. Tetherow, Wagon Train Master. Portland: Fred Lockley, undated.

Lockley, Fred. Conversations with Bullwhackers, Muleskinners, Etc. Eugene, Oregon: Rainy Day Press, 1981.

Lockley, Fred. Conversations with Pioneer Women. Eugene, Oregon: Rainy Day Press, 1981.

Lockley, Fred. History of the Columbia River Valley from The Dalles to the Sea, Volume I. Chicago: S. J. Clarke Publishing Company.

Lockley, Fred. " A Legend of the Alseas". Oregon Teachers Monthly,

February, 1903, pp. 22-24.

Long, R. A. and E. R. Jackman. The Oregon Desert. Caldwell, Idaho: The Caxton Printers, 1964.

Lopez, Barry Holstun. Giving Birth to Thunder, Sleeping with His Daughter. Kansas City: Sheed Andrews and McMeal, Inc., 1977.

Lyman, H. S. History of Oregon: The Growth of an American State. New York: North Pacific Publishing Society, 1903.

Lyman, H. S. "The Indian Arabian Nights". The Pacific Monthly, Volume II. May, 1899-October, 1899, pp. 219-221.

Lyman, H. S. "The Indian Arabian Nights". The Pacific Monthly, Volume III, November, 1899-April 1900.

Lyman, H. S. "Indian Legends and How I Came By Them". Oregon Teachers Monthly, February, 1904, pp. 28-32.

Lyman, H. S. "Indian Legends and How I Got Them, Part I. Oregon Teachers Monthly, December, 1903, pp. 15-20.

Lyman, H. S. "Indian Legends and How I Got Them, Part II. Oregon Teachers Monthly, January, 1904, pp. 13-17.

Lyman, H. S. "Reminiscences of Louis Labonte". Oregon Historical Society Quarterly, Volume I, 1900, pp. 169-188.

Lyman, W. D. The Columbia River: Its History, Its Myths, Its Scenery, Its Commerce. New York: The Knickerbocker Press, 1909.

Lyman, W. D. "Indian Myths of Mount Adams". Mazama, December, 1913, pp. 14-17.

Lyman, W. D. Indian Myths of the Northwest. Worcester, Massachusetts: American Antiquarian Society, 1915.

Lyman, W. D. "Legends of the Cascades". The Mountaineer, Volume III,

November, 1910, pp. 40-43.

Lyman, W. D. "Rainier Indian Legends". Mazama, December, 1905, pp. 203-207.

Martin, Jim. "Indian legend explains why the ocean roars". The Sunday Oregonian, December 13, 1976.

Maynard, Madge. "The Legend of Joseph Lake". Oregon Teachers Monthly, September, 1904, pp. 12-13.

Maynard, Madge. "The Seven Devils". Oregon Teachers Monthly, May, 1905, p. 9.

Maynard, Madge. "The Story of Wallowa". Oregon Teachers Monthly, October, 1904, pp. 10-11.

McClure, Andrew S. The Diary of Andrew S. McClure, 1829-1898. Eugene, Oregon: Lane County Historical Society, 1973.

McClure, John Hamilton. How We Came to Oregon. (including the Bruce genealogy and the Diary of James F. McClure.) Eugene, Oregon: Lane County Historical Society, 1967.

McNary, Lawrence A. "Route of the Meek Cut-off, 1845". Oregon Historical Quarterly, Volume 35, Number 1, March, 1934.

Meek, Stephen Hall, The Autobiography of a Mountain Man. Pasadena, California: Glen Dawson, 1948. (First published as "A Sketch of Life of the First Pioneer", in The Golden Era, April, 1885 p. 9)

Melvin, George. "The Rivers of Oregon: The M'Kinzie". The Pacific Monthly, Volume III, #4, February, 1900.

Miller, Emma Gene. Clatsop County, Oregon. Portland, Oregon: Binfords & Mort, 1958.

Miller, Joaquin. "The Legend of Mt. Shasta". The Pacific Monthly, Volume IV, May-October, 1900.

Murie, Adolph. Ecology of the Coyote in the Yellowstone. Washington, DC: US Government Printing Office, 1940.

Owen, Benjamin Franklin. My Trip Across the Plains, March-October, 1853. Eugene, Oregon: Lane County Historical Society, 1967.

"Oregon Oddities". Oregon Writers Project and Historical Records Survey of the Works Progress Administration.

Packard, R. L. "Notes on the Mythology and Religion of the Nez Perces". Journal of American Folklore, Volume IV. Published for the American Folklore Society by Houghton, Mifflin and Company, 1891. Reprinted by Kraus Reprint Corporation, 1963.

Petley, Claudia. "The Legend of the Sacred Heart", The Pacific Monthly, Volume VII, January-June, 1902.

Powell, Mary E. "The Legends of Nehalem". North Cost Times Eagle, Wheeler, Oregon, January 15, 1976.

Powers, Alfred. Legends of the Four High Mountains. Portland: Junior Historical Journal, 1944.

Putnam, George Palmer. In the Oregon Country. New York: G. P. Putnam's Sons, 1915.

Ramsey, Jarold, editor. Coyote Was Going There. Seattle: University of Washington Press, 1977.

Ranck, Glen. "Tribal Lore of Wisham Indians Rich in Traditions of Columbia". The Oregonian, February 7, 1926, section 3, page 9.

Reid, Charles B. "Washougal, An Indian Romance". The Pacific Monthly, Volume II, May-October, 1899.

Roberts, Ella P. "Lost Lake". Mazama, Volume VI, #1, December, 1920, pp. 79-81.

Robertson, Lance, "Coburg Hills old growth to be cut". The Register Guard, Eugene, February 21, 1990, p. C1.

Rogers, Thomas H. "Captain Tugg and the Pirates' Treasure Chamber". Oregon Native Son, Volume I, #3, January, 1900.

Rogers, Thomas H. "North Pacific Prehistoric Wrecks". Oregon Native Son, Volume II, #1, May 1900, pp. 219-227.

Ruby, Robert H. and John A. Brown. The Cayuse Indians: Imperial Tribesmen of Old Oregon. University of Oklahoma Press, 1972.

Sapir, Edward. Wishram Texts, together with Wasco Tales and Myths. (collected by Jeremiah Curtin) Leyden: Publications of the American Ethnological Society, edited by Franz Boas, 1909.

Saylor, F. H. "The Bridge of the Gods". Oregon Native Son, Volume I, #3, January, 1900, pp. 417-423.

Saylor, F. H. "Legendary Lore of the Indians". Oregon Native Son, Volume II, #1, May, 1900.

Saylor, F. H. "Legend of Snake River Valley". Oregon Native Son, Volume II, #1, May 1900, pp. 15-19.

Saylor, F. H. "The Legend of Tahoma". Oregon Native Son, Volume I, #6, October, 1899, pp. 315-316.

Saylor, F. H. "Multnomah: A Tradition". Oregon Native Son, Volume I, #10, March, 1900, pp. 525-530.

Saylor, F. H. "The Multnomah's Last Signal Fire" and "Legend of Mt. Shasta". Oregon Native Son, Volume I, #4, August, 1899. pp. 183-187.

Saylor, F. H. "Speelyia: A Legend of the Formation of Latourelle Falls and the Pillars of Hercules". The Pacific Monthly, Volume VII, January-June, 1902.

Schnebly, Lillian May. "The Origin of the Tribes". The Pacific Monthly,

Volume V, November, 1900-May, 1901.

Sicade, Henry. "Aboriginal Nomenclature." <u>Mazama</u>, December, 1918, pp. 251-254.

Smith, Elva J. "Dead Indian Lake". <u>Oregon Teachers Monthly</u>, September, 1904, pp. 19-20.

Smith, Elva J. "The Duel of the Mountains", <u>Oregon Teachers Monthly</u>, May, 1904, pp. 21-22.

Smith, Elva J. "The Legend of Coolca's Pillar". <u>Oregon Teachers Monthly</u>, November, 1904, pp. 18-19.

Smith, Elva J. "Multnomah". <u>Oregon Teachers Monthly</u>, February, 1904, p. 9.

Smith, Elva J. "The Sacrifice". <u>Oregon Teachers Monthly</u>, September, 1912, pp. 4-6.

Smith, Elva J. "The Origin of Man". <u>Oregon Teachers Monthly</u>, October, 1904, p. 13.

Smith, Silas B. "Tales of early wrecks on the Oregon Coast and how the Beeswax got there". <u>Oregon Native Son</u>, Volume I, #3, January, 1900, pp. 443-446.

Smith, Silas B. "A Legend of the Surf". <u>Oregon Teachers Monthly</u>, February, 1905, pp. 29-30.

Steel, William Gladstone, "Legend of the Llaos". <u>Steel Points</u>, Volume I, #2, January, 1907.

Stern, Bernhard J. <u>The Lummi Indians of Northwest Washington</u>. New York: Columbia University Press, 1934.

Stillman, A. D. "Eastern Oregon Indians. <u>Oregon Native Son</u>, Volume I, #3, July, 1899.

Stinsman, E. Stanley. "How the Salmon Came to the Frazier River". Manuscript in Oregon Collection, University of Oregon Library.

Stokes, Ted. "Indian George, hounds remembered on Halloween". The Sunday Oregonian, October 27, 1974, p. A-37.

Strycker, Lisa, "Cyanide mines worry conservationists". The Register Guard, Eugene, October 8, 1989, p. 1A.

Vickery, Jim Dale. Wilderness Visionaries. Merrillville, Indiana: ICS Books, Inc., 1986.

Vincent, Fred W. "Indian Gods Dug Columbia Gorge". Northwest Living Magazine, Oregon Journal. August 19, 1956.

Waggoner, George A. Stories of Old Oregon. Salem: Statesman Publishing Company, 1905.

Weatherson, Mr. and Mrs. W. H. a letter to George H. Hines of the Oregon Historical Society, dated May 14, 1923.

Wells, Harry L. Multnomah: A Legend of the Columbia. Portland: Kilham's, 1923.

Wood, Charles Erskine Scott. A Book of Tales, being some myths of the North American Indians. New York: The Vanguard Press, 1929.

Wood, T. A. "Beauty, Beeswax and Rum. The first Landing on the North Pacific Coast, An Indian Tradition". Oregon Native Son, Volume I, #6, October, 1899, pp. 299-301.

Young, Stanley P. and Hartley H. T. Jackson. The Clever Coyote. Lincoln, Nebraska: University of Nebraska Press. 1978.

Acknowledgments

A one-horse publishing outfit like Rainy Day Press would never finish anything without a great deal of help. I would like to thank the following special people who helped to make this book possible:

Bill Butler, Tim Joyce, and the many others who greeted me with kindness, hospitality, and assistance as I traveled in search of Coyote;

Chris Helm for reading and listening to the countless variations this book assumed before it was committed to this form, and for proofreading and editing the text, and for drawing the maps;

Polly Ann Helm, my daughter, for carving the coyote for the cover and the owl on page 194, for proofreading and editing the text, and for labeling the maps;

Tom Layton, computer wizard, for never being too busy to explain again how to make this marvelous machine do my bidding.

Chris, Luke, Malindi, and Polly Helm for our adventures in the Blue Goose.

The Oregon Country Library

1. Conversations with Pioneer Women
By Fred Lockley, compiled and edited by Mike Helm. 310 pages.

2. Conversations with Bullwhackers, Muleskinners, Pioneers, Prospectors, '49ers, Indian Fighters, Trappers, Ex-Barkeepers, Authors, Preachers, Poets & Near Poets & All Sorts & Conditions of Men
By Fred Lockley, compiled and edited by Mike Helm. 358 pages.

3. Visionaries, Mountain Men and Empire Builders
By Fred Lockley, compiled and edited by Mike Helm. 395 pages.

4. A Bit of Verse: Poetry (&Etc.) from the Lockley Files
By Fred Lockley, compiled and edited by Mike Helm. 165 pages.

5. Oregon's Ghosts and Monsters
By Mike Helm. 158 pages.

6. Tracking Down Coyote
By Mike Helm. 218 pages.

What they say about the Oregon Country Library:
"...an amazing oral history collection..."
Small Press Review
"...engaging, meaningful documentation of women's experiences on the frontier..."
Seattle Post Intelligencer
"...preserves something today's Oregonians forget at their peril—the human dimension."
Corvallis Gazette-Times
"...enough colorful wind to sail a ship."
Portland Oregonian
"...highly recommended."
Kliatt Paperback Book Guide
"...a rare treasure..."
Corvallis Gazette Times
"I highly recommend this book."
Wyoming Library Roundup
"...vivid view of those obscure lives..."
Western Humanities Review

A special offer for lovers
of Pacific Northwest Literature
The Oregon Country Library

Please send me:

_____copies of **Conversations with Pioneer Women,**
  $13.95 each $_____

_____copies of **Conversations with Bullwhackers, Etc.,**
  $11.95 each $_____

_____copies of **Visionaries, Mountain Men & Empire Builders,**
  $15.95 each $_____

_____copies of **A Bit of Verse: Poems, (& Etc.) from the Lockley Files**
  $7.95 each $_____

_____copies of **Oregon's Ghosts and Monsters,**
  $8.95 each $_____

_____copies of **Tracking Down Coyote,**
  $14.95 each $_____

                              subtotal $_____

                 Less discount of 10%   -$_____

Plus postage & Handling $_____
($1.20 for the first book, $.40 for each additional book)

                       Total enclosed $_____

Name_____Address_____

City_____State_____Zip_____

Rainy Day Press
PO Box 3035
Eugene, OR 97403